27

Colour
Encyclopedia
of the
World

Mustering sheep against a background of towering mountains at Glentanner Station, Canterbury South Island

Colour Encyclopedia of the World

Euan & Kate Sutherland
revised by Antony Kamm

WARD LOCK LIMITED LONDON

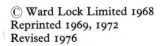

ISBN 0 7063 1171 X

First published in Great Britain in 1968
by Ward Lock Limited, 116 Baker Street,
London, W1M 2BB

Text filmset in 11pt. Plantin
by Servis Filmsetting, Manchester

Printed and bound by
Toppan Printing Company, Singapore

Contents

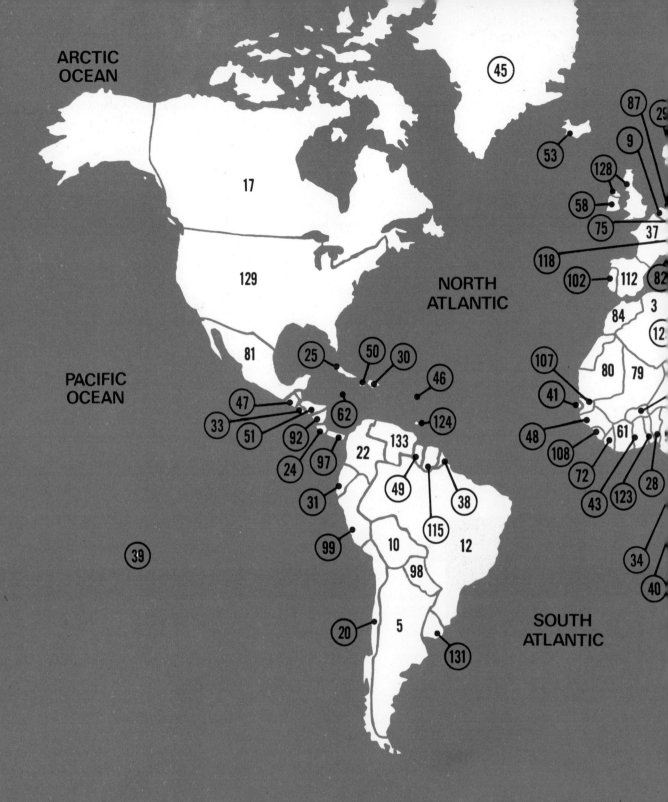

ARCTIC
OCEAN

NORTH
ATLANTIC

PACIFIC
OCEAN

SOUTH
ATLANTIC

1	Afghanistan	19	Chad	37	France	55	Indonesia
2	Albania	20	Chile	38	French Guiana	56	Iran (Persia)
3	Algeria	21	China	39	French Polynesia	57	Iraq
4	Angola	22	Colombia	40	Gabon	58	Irish Republic (Eire)
5	Argentina	23	Congo People's Republic	41	Gambia	59	Israel
6	Australia	24	Costa Rica	42	Germany	60	Italy
7	Austria	25	Cuba	43	Ghana	61	Ivory Coast
8	Bangladesh	26	Cyprus	44	Greece	62	Jamaica
9	Belgium	27	Czechoslovakia	45	Greenland	63	Japan
10	Bolivia	28	Dahomey	46	Guadeloupe	64	Jordan
11	Botswana	29	Denmark	47	Guatemala	65	Kenya
12	Brazil	30	Dominican Republic	48	Guinea	66	Khmer Republic
13	Bulgaria	31	Ecuador	49	Guyana		(Cambodia)
14	Burma	32	Egypt	50	Haiti	67	Korea
15	Burundi	33	El Salvador	51	Honduras	68	Kuwait
16	Cameroun	34	Equatorial Guinea	52	Hungary	69	Laos
17	Canada	35	Ethiopia	53	Iceland	70	Lebanon
18	Central African Republic	36	Finland	54	India		

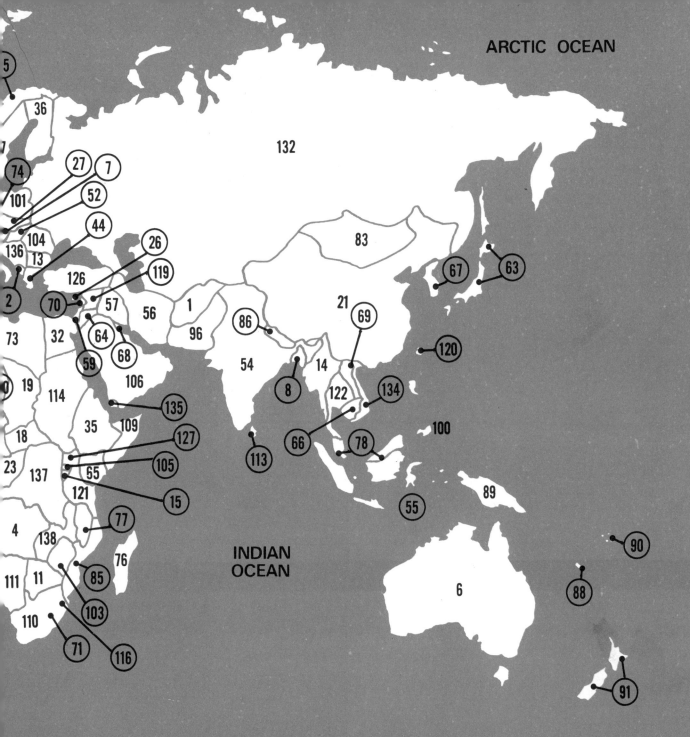

ARCTIC OCEAN

132

INDIAN
OCEAN

THE WORLD

71	Lesotho	88	New Caledonia	105	Ruanda	122	Thailand (Siam)
72	Liberia	89	New Guinea	106	Saudi Arabia	123	Togo
73	Libya	90	New Hebrides	107	Senegal	124	Trinidad and Tobago
74	Liechtenstein	91	New Zealand	108	Sierra Leone	125	Tunisia
75	Luxembourg	92	Nicaragua	109	Somali Republic	126	Turkey
76	Malagasy Republic	93	Niger	110	South Africa	127	Uganda
77	Malawi	94	Nigeria	111	S.W. Africa (Namibia)	128	United Kingdom
78	Malaysia	95	Norway	112	Spain	129	United States
79	Mali	96	Pakistan	113	Sri Lanka	130	Upper Volta
80	Mauritania	97	Panama	114	Sudan	131	Uruguay
81	Mexico	98	Paraguay	115	Surinam	132	U.S.S.R.
82	Monaco	99	Peru	116	Swaziland (Ngwane)	133	Venezuela
83	Mongolia	100	Philippines	117	Sweden	134	Vietnam
84	Morocco	101	Poland	118	Switzerland	135	Yemen
85	Mozambique	102	Portugal	119	Syria	136	Yugoslavia
86	Nepal	103	Rhodesia	120	Taiwan (Formosa)	137	Zaire
87	Netherlands	104	Romania	121	Tanzania	138	Zambia

Preface

The purpose of Colour Encyclopedia of the World is simply to present the most significant features of the geography of our earth and its many and varied peoples. Such knowledge will not only lead to a deeper appreciation of our world in all its manifold beauty but to that mutual understanding of races which is so important in a world too often plagued by racial strife.

In a work of this size the editors have had to be selective and approach their subjects from different points of view; sometimes from the standpoint of geography, at other times with the eye of the economist, and often historically. An additional factor is the magnificent colour photographs which so profusely illustrate the text. The total result, so the editors hope, is a world picture of man on earth.

The world's population is expanding so rapidly, and with it the number of factories, towns and industries in general, that one of the greatest problems we have to face is that of pollution of the earth, sea and air by chemicals, industrial waste and so on; together with the rapid diminution of the wild areas in every country, with the resulting loss of plant and animal life. Most nations now have extensive conservation programmes, and efforts are being made to save wild animals which are in danger of extinction as well as to preserve the countryside and keep rivers, lakes and seas clean and free from pollution so that marine life can flourish.

A work of this nature could not be compiled without access to official information, and the editors would like to express their sincere thanks to the embassy officials of all the countries dealt with in this book for so generously making available such information. Any opinions expressed in the text are, however, solely the responsibility of the editors.

Oceania

AUSTRALIA
Nation in Commonwealth
Area: 7,687,000 sq. km/2,968,000 sq. miles
Population: 13,100,000   Capital: Canberra
Flag: Blue ground with Union Jack against mast and 6 white stars

Australia is the world's largest island. Of its total area about a third has a tropical climate with warm winters and hot summers. Much of Australia is desert, dry and completely without water; lack of water supplies was one of Australia's major problems in exploiting her agriculture, crops and animals needing plentiful and regular supplies of water to survive. The discovery of useful minerals in the desert areas provided an alternative source of revenue and the great hydro schemes provide water for the areas still needing it. The population of Australia is very small in proportion to its area. The vast majority of the population are English-speaking immigrants; over twelve million are of European origin and the remainder are aborigines and Chinese.

Australia became an island very early in geological times and as a result many unique animals and plants have developed. Since no other land surface has been exposed to the same influences, the land area, and particularly the more fertile eastern area, has many interesting aspects. The most famous Australian animals are the marsupials, that is, animals that bring forth their young in an incomplete stage of development and rear them in a pouch. The best known of these animals are the koala and kangaroo, the latter being the emblem of the country. The country is roughly divisible into

Ayers Rock near Alice Springs in central Australia. This landscape of desert and scrub is typical of the central and western regions of Australia

9

The koala bear, found only in Australia, which lives on eucalyptus leaves

Herding a flock of sheep in Australia

A typical Australian farm near Broken Hill, New South Wales

two parts, the fertile east and the less fertile west. In the east for some considerable distance inland there is intensive farming, particularly sheep and dairy farming, both forming important parts of Australia's exports. Australia's major exports are farm and mineral products. Wool, meat, wheat and now manufactured goods as well are all exported. Although wool is the staple product of Australia, supplying a third of all the world's wool, great increases are also being made in the production of other crops. Cotton and rice are now being developed to meet the nation's needs.

In the west of Australia the country is arid and desert like. It is here that the great cattle ranches support nearly thirty million head of cattle, on dry country that, until the discovery of minerals, could not be used for anything else. The mineral deposits of the eastern region are considerable. Australia is the world's largest producer of lead and the third largest producer of zinc, as well as a major source of iron ore, copper and bauxite. Japan is a major

customer for the iron ore produced, and at Port Pirie in South Australia is the world's largest refinery for lead. It has a capacity of two hundred thousand tonnes a year. Australian industry already makes use of a considerable proportion of the mineral wealth of the country. The manufacturing industry employs over a quarter of the country's work force, producing for the home consumer market and for the export trade. About 6 per cent of this work force is employed in the motor industry. The car industry has developed at great speed to feed the ever expanding market as new roads are finished all over the country. In such a large country transport is of very great importance and there is approximately one car for every two people in the country.

One of the major sources of increased power in Australia is the Snowy Mountains Scheme in New South Wales. This hydro-electric scheme is one of the largest in the world. The scheme produces two things essential to Australia's developing industry,

I N D O N E S I A

IRIAN
JAYA

Jakarta
Semarang
Surabaya
JAVA
Bali
Jogjakarta
SUMBAWA
SUMBA
FLORES
TIMOR
ARAFURA SEA

Carpe

TIMOR SEA

Darwin

ARNHEM LAND

Daly

Victoria

KIMBERLEY

I N D I A N

BARKLY TABLELAND

DAMPIER
LAND

Fitzroy
Fitzroy

NORTHERN

Port Hedland

Eighty Mile Beach

Great Sandy

TERRITORY

Georgina

Desert

Barrow
Creek

De Grey

O C E A N

Fortescue

Sandover

Hamersley Range

Ashburton

Gibson Desert

Alice
Springs

Simpson

Macdonnell Ranges

Desert

Gascoyne

Petermann
Ranges

Alberga

Carnarvon

WESTERN AUSTRALIA

Musgrave
Ranges

Warburt

L.
Eyre

Coopers

Great Victoria Desert

Stuart
Range

SOUTH AUSTRALIA

Geraldton

L.
Torrens

L.
Gairdner

Flinde

Woomera

Kalgoorlie

NULLARBOR PLAIN

Port
Augu

Perth

Port
Piri

Fremantle

Great Australian

Bunbury

Bight

Adelaide

Albany

0		500		1000 *miles*

0	500	1000	1500 *kilometres*

Australia and New Zealand

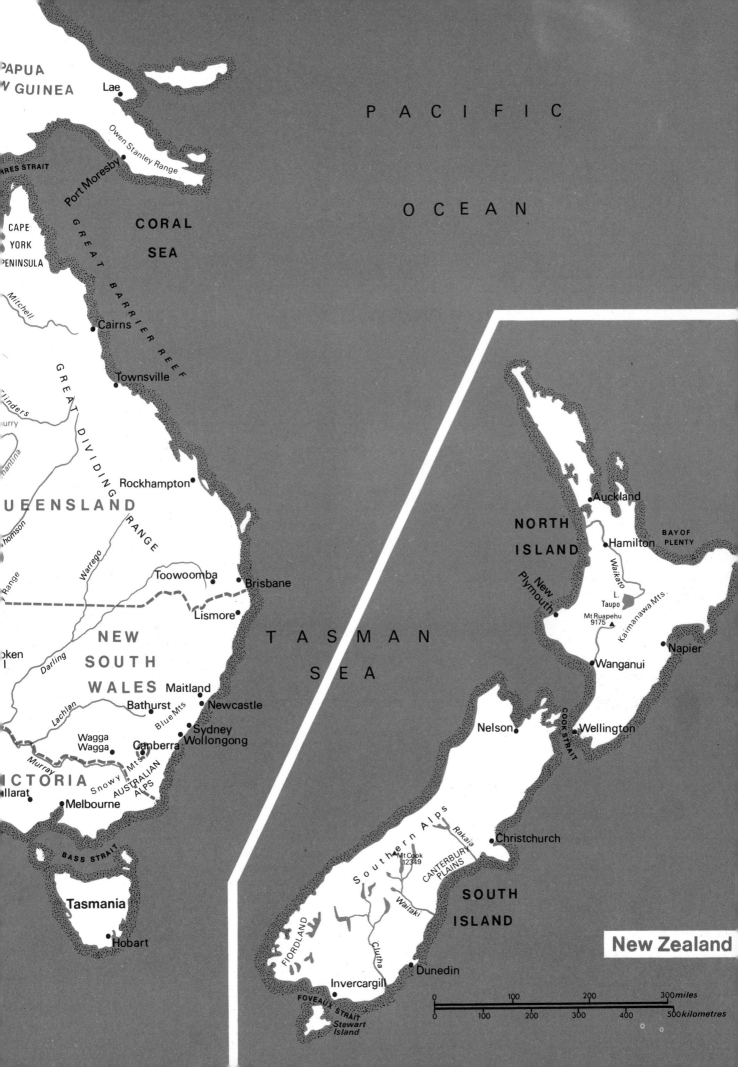

PAPUA
NEW GUINEA

Lae

Owen Stanley Range

Port Moresby

TRES STRAIT

CAPE
YORK
PENINSULA

Mitchell

CORAL
SEA

GREAT BARRIER REEF

PACIFIC

OCEAN

Cairns

GREAT

Flinders

urry

Townsville

DIVIDING

Rockhampton

QUEENSLAND

RANGE

homson

Warrego

Range

Toowoomba

Brisbane

Lismore

ken
l

Darling

NEW

SOUTH

WALES

Maitland

Lachlan

Bathurst

Blue Mts

Newcastle

Wagga
Wagga

Canberra

Sydney
Wollongong

Murray

Snowy Mts

AUSTRALIAN
ALPS

CTORIA

larat

Melbourne

BASS STRAIT

Tasmania

Hobart

TASMAN

SEA

NORTH

ISLAND

Auckland

Hamilton

BAY OF
PLENTY

New
Plymouth

Waikato

L.
Taupo

Kaimanawa Mts.

Mt Ruapehu
9175

Napier

Wanganui

Nelson

COOK STRAIT

Wellington

Southern Alps

Rakaia

Christchurch

Mt Cook
12349

CANTERBURY
PLAINS

SOUTH

ISLAND

Waitaki

FIORDLAND

Clutha

New Zealand

Dunedin

Invercargill

FOVEAUX STRAIT

Stewart
Island

0   100   200   300 miles

0   100   200   300   400   500 kilometres

A view over Sydney Harbour, showing the famous bridge and the white, winged roof of the Opera House

power from the hydro schemes which provides cheap power for industry and water and irrigation from the dams which increases the productivity of the land and makes possible the cultivation of greater areas of land. Nuclear power has not yet been introduced on a commercial basis.

Australia's climate, which poses these problems of water shortage in many areas, also makes the country one of the most pleasant places in the world to live. Around the coastal areas, especially in the south and east, the temperate climate provides warmth and sunshine all the year round. The coastline is now a series of holiday resorts which are in use all the year round as the large population of the cities drives out to relax by the sea after working in the towns all week. More than half the total population lives in the six capital cities of the six states of Australia: Sydney, Brisbane, Adelaide, Perth, Melbourne and Hobart. In spite of the fact that so many Australians are town dwellers, they spend enough time in the open air to become famous all over the world as magnificent sportsmen, especially in cricket, swimming and tennis; certainly the combination of food, sun and fresh air which all Australians get is of great importance in their success at sport, but another factor is their competitive attitude to sport at all levels.

Education is compulsory from five to fifteen and there are fifteen universities, providing courses in all subjects. Social security benefits are provided for all Australians – there are old-age pensions, widows pensions, maternity allowances and children's allowances for children of school age. There are unemployment and sickness benefits, and hospital benefits for those who need treatment in hospital. For people with tuberculosis there are special rates, though the numbers of tuberculosis patients is declining rapidly as the standard of living increases. These benefits provide the Australian with an assurance that when he is in need there is some money available to help him.

Europeans were not the first to settle in Australia. They were preceded by the aborigines some fifteen thousand years ago. These people until only a few years ago lived in a way not very different from that of primitive man some twenty thousand years ago. In recent years many have taken to Western ways of living, working as ranch hands on cattle farms, but a few tribes still follow a traditional way of life in the Northern Territory, especially in Arnhem Land and the central desert region.

NEW ZEALAND
Nation in Commonwealth
Area: 269,000 sq. km/104,000 sq. miles
Population: 3,000,000   Capital: Wellington
Flag: Blue ground with Union Jack against mast and 4 white stars with red centres

New Zealand consists of a number of islands of varying sizes in the South Pacific Ocean. The largest two, known as North and South Island, contain the vast majority of New Zealand's population and activities. The smaller islands are widely dispersed over a large area of the ocean from 8 degrees south to 60 degrees south. New Zealand also has a considerable interest in Antarctica and is one of the signatories of a treaty agreeing to exploit Antarctica for peaceful purposes only. A large amount of the area of New Zealand, especially in

New Zealand indigenous bush country in Auckland, North Island

North Island, is mountainous. There are also in North Island the geysers and hot springs for which New Zealand is famous. The rivers, although rich in fish, are too short and rapid for navigation. The South Island contains the Canterbury plains on which graze the vast quantities of sheep which account for a large proportion of New Zealand's overseas exports. Sheep and wool are the major products of New Zealand's farmers. There are over

15

Cattle grazing on the rich pastures at the foot of Mount Taramaki, North Island

Geo Thermal bores at Warnakei. The steam caused by volcanic activity is harnessed to provide domestic heat and electricity

60 million sheep in New Zealand. Counting sheep and cattle together, there are some 24 times as many animals in the country as there are people. The success of New Zealand's agricultural industry was ensured when in 1882 the ship *Dunedin* set sail from Wellington, with the first cargo of refrigerated meat. Mineral production in New Zealand is relatively small and gold mining, which was until recently an important source of wealth, has declined considerably. Coal is the main source of mineral wealth. The other minerals which are mined in fairly small quantities are copper, silver, iron ore, manganese ore, tungsten and asbestos.

New Zealand's comparatively small population means that the resources of the country are seldom strained, space and jobs are plentiful, and the standard of living is as high as that of Canada and Australia. The climate is mild and moist and relatively unchanging throughout the year – a great advantage to farming since it allows several crops to be grown within a single year. Very little snow falls on the lower ground even in the South Island, except on the heights of the New Zealand Alps where the snow is sufficiently heavy to act as a training ground for Himalayan expeditions.

Like Australia, New Zealand has an indigenous population, the Maoris. These are a people of Polynesian stock who live mainly on North Island, having emigrated there from Rarotonga about the middle of the fourteenth century. Although there was strife when Britain took over the islands in the nineteenth century, the Maoris have integrated remarkably well. They follow a Western way of life but they still preserve many of their old traditions, especially war chants and dances, as anyone will know who has been to a New Zealand rugby football match.

ANTARCTICA
Area: 5,000,000 sq. miles/12,000,000 sq. km
Antarctica is the most recently discovered continent in the world. For centuries people merely presumed that there was a mass in the southern part of the globe that balanced the land mass they already knew of in the north, and it was not until the seventeenth century that the more daring explorers began to search for this Unknown South Land as they called it. Abel Tasman, who discovered New Zealand in 1642, thought that these islands might

be the northern part of this continent, but this was finally disproved when Captain James Cook sailed all the way round New Zealand in the late eighteenth century. Cook was the first known person to sail south of the Antarctic Circle, but it was not until a further fifty years had passed that the first land south of the circle was sighted. This was what is now called Peter I Island, discovered by the Russian Admiral Bellingshausen.

The first sighting of the Antarctic continent, so far as we know – for it is possible that sailors had seen the continent earlier than this but either did not realize what they saw or never returned to tell the tale – was in January 1820. At that time the northern part of the great Antarctic peninsula was sighted by the ship's company of the brig *Williams* and her master, Capt. Edward Bransfield, R.N. After this, many other parts of the continent were viewed by sealing boats and naval vessels. A very important discovery, from the point of view of landing on Antarctica and exploring inland, was made by Capt. James Clark Ross in 1841. With his two ships, Ross broke through the pack ice that bars the approach to Antarctica from all sides, discovered the mountainous part of the north-east Victoria Land and continued to sail southward until his path was barred by the solid wall of ice now known as the Ross Ice Shelf. This part of the ocean, named the Ross Sea after its finder, cuts deep into the continent and was to be used time and again by Antarctic explorers as the best beginning for an attempt to reach the Pole.

The sailors who made these first expeditions must have gone through considerable hardship, and for very little reward. Even if they succeeded in forcing a ship through the pack-ice, they then had to negotiate a sea full of icebergs, some of them of great length, rising 30m (100 ft) out of the water. They were probably pleasantly surprised, however, to find how much wild life there was. The most characteristically Antarctic of these are the penguins. Some of the Emperor penguins are as much as 1·2m (4 ft) tall, weighing 45 kg (100 lb). More common are the smaller Adelie penguins, which can be seen on all parts of the coast. There are Weddell seals to be seen, lying on the ice or asleep on an ice-flow, and it is here too that killer whales can be seen hunting.

In 1895 the first known landing was made on the

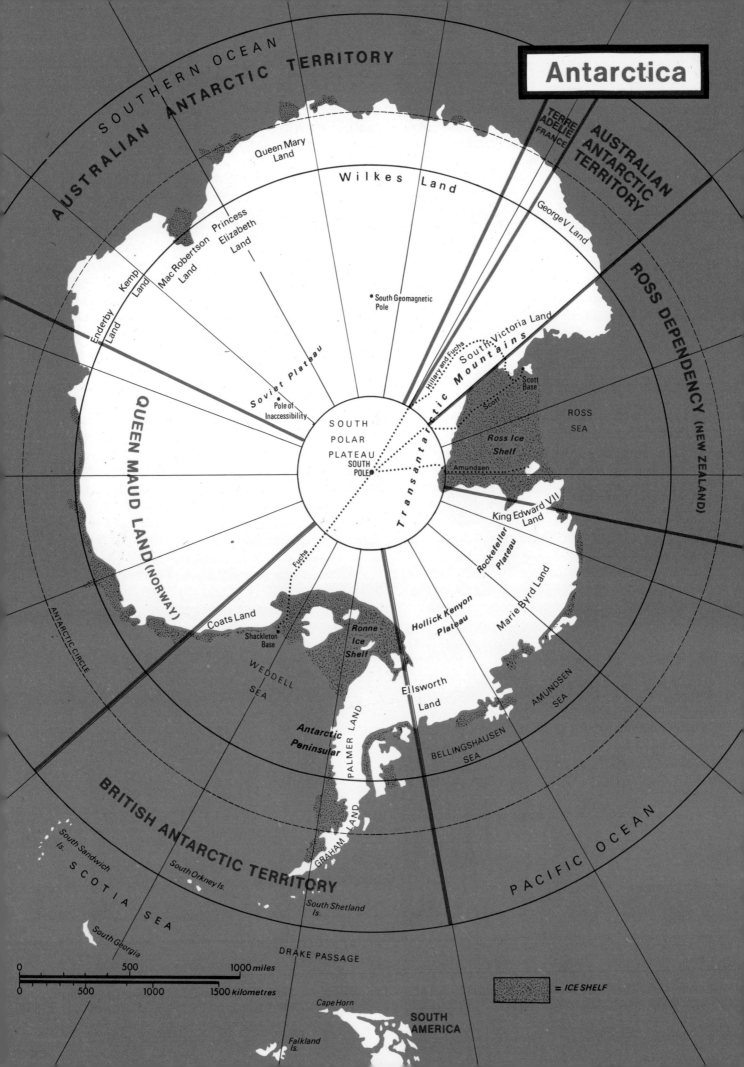

Antarctica

SOUTHERN OCEAN

AUSTRALIAN ANTARCTIC TERRITORY

TERRE ADELIE FRANCE

AUSTRALIAN ANTARCTIC TERRITORY

ROSS DEPENDENCY (NEW ZEALAND)

Queen Mary Land

Wilkes Land

George V Land

Princess Elizabeth Land

Mac Robertson Land

Kemp Land

Enderby Land

South Geomagnetic Pole

Soviet Plateau

Pole of Inaccessibility

South Victoria Land

Hillary and Fuchs

Transantarctic Mountains

Scott Base

Scott

SOUTH POLAR PLATEAU

SOUTH POLE

ROSS SEA

Ross Ice Shelf

Amundsen

QUEEN MAUD LAND (NORWAY)

King Edward VII Land

Rockefeller Plateau

Marie Byrd Land

Fuchs

Coats Land

Shackleton Base

Hollick Kenyon Plateau

Ronne Ice Shelf

Ellsworth Land

AMUNDSEN SEA

ANTARCTIC CIRCLE

WEDDELL SEA

PALMER LAND

Antarctic Peninsular

BELLINGSHAUSEN SEA

PACIFIC OCEAN

BRITISH ANTARCTIC TERRITORY

GRAHAM LAND

South Sandwich Is.

SCOTIA SEA

South Orkney Is.

South Shetland Is.

South Georgia

DRAKE PASSAGE

| 0 | 500 | 1000 *miles* |

| 0 | 500 | 1000 | 1500 *kilometres* |

= *ICE SHELF*

Cape Horn

SOUTH AMERICA

Falkland Is.

Antarctic mainland by a Norwegian, J. H. Bull, from a wooden sailing boat, and then, in 1901, the first exploratory expedition set out, led by Robert Falcon Scott. Their ship, the *Discovery*, was moored in McMurdo Sound and allowed to be frozen in, and the crew of fifty lived here throughout the Antarctic winter. In November 1902, three of the party, Scott, Dr. Wilson and Lieut. Shackleton, began to sledge south over the ice shelf. They knew little about sledging and, in consequence, the dogs they had brought to pull the sledges soon began to fail, and the men had to haul the sledges themselves. They travelled south in this way for 610 km (380 miles), and still saw no sign of the ice-shelf coming to an end, but now their food was running out and Shackleton was ill. They had to turn back, and at the end of thirty-four days, at last reached the ship.

In January 1903, a relief ship had arrived, and she was able to take Shackleton and several other members of the crew away, but the *Discovery* was stuck so fast in the ice that Scott and the rest of the men decided that they would have to spend another winter there. This at least gave them the chance to explore further during the next summer. Scott and

two others ascended the Farrar Glacier and sledged across the high plateau for some 320 km (200 miles). The *Discovery* was at last freed at the beginning of 1904.

In spite of his fearful experiences on the earlier expedition, Shackleton was determined to return to Antarctica and try again to get nearer the Pole. This time a hut was built, not far from where the *Discovery* had wintered, for Shackleton and his fourteen companions to live in. Their ship returned to New Zealand for the winter.

Shackleton set out with Adams and Wild along the same route that he had followed with Scott, and for a time made excellent progress. This time, instead of dogs, he had four Manchurian ponies to draw the sledges. Within a month they had passed the point where Scott had had to turn back, but soon they noticed the mountains that separated them from the high plateau which they would have to reach if they were to get to the Pole. The only way they could cross this chain was by ascending a glacier – now known as the Beardmore Glacier. This was a perilous ascent, and their last remaining pony fell down a crevass and was lost, so that in addition to everything else, the men had to pull their own

Adelie penguins on a rocky foreland overlooking pack ice and icebergs

sledges. Nevertheless, they reached the top, and the great flat plain of ice that lies 3,000m (10,000 ft) above sea level. They were now not far from the Pole, but their food was running perilously short, and with only 157 km (97 miles) to go, they were compelled to turn back. Even so, it was not certain that they would be able to reach base, so weakened were they by very hard labour on very little food. Sometimes they had only one biscuit a meal, and if they had missed one of the food depots they had left on the outward journey, they would have starved. In the end, Shackleton and Wild had to make a desperate march to base and send out a rescue party to pick up the other two.

Scott returned to the Antarctic in the ship *Terra Nova* in January 1911. Parties were sent out to prepare depots for the big journey to the Pole. Meanwhile it was discovered that on the other side of the Ross Sea another party had landed with the intention of racing to the Pole. This expedition was led by the Norwegian, Roald Amundsen.

Scott's main attempt began in November 1911. He set out with a party of sixteen, two motor sledges, ten ponies and two dog teams. The motors soon broke down and the dog teams had to turn back at the foot of the Beardmore Glacier. The ponies eventually had to be shot. By the time the expedition reached the Polar Plateau it consisted only of eight men hauling two sledges, and shortly afterwards the last supporting party of three left the other five to make the attempt over the last lap, with the Pole still about 210 km (130 miles) away. This was on the 5th January. By the 14th they were 65 km (40 miles) from the finish, but on the 16th it was clear that they could never be the first people to reach the Pole. There, in their path, fluttered a black flag, left by Amundsen before them, and, when they reached the Pole two days later they found a note left for them by Amundsen.

The journey home was made up of one disaster after another. As they were descending the glacier, Evans fell, suffered concussion, and died within a few hours. The party then moved slowly across the Ice Shelf, weak with sickness and hunger. One of the party, Oates, had badly frostbitten feet, so that he was unable to pull the sledge at all, and, knowing that he was holding the others up, he walked out of his tent into a blizzard one night and was never seen

A scientific research base in Antarctica

A cliff of solid ice in Antarctica

again. On 19th March the remaining three were only 18 km (11 miles) from One Ton Depot, where there was plenty of food and fuel, but at this point they were struck by a blizzard. They were confined to their tents as day after day passed, and soon they were too weak to move, even if the blizzard had let up. They all wrote farewell letters to their friends, and Scott put down his memorable Message to the Public: 'We are weak, writing is difficult, but for

my own sake I do not regret this journey. Had we lived, I should have had a tale to tell of the hardihood, endurance and courage of my companions which would have stirred the heart of every Englishman. These rough notes and our dead bodies must tell this tale.'

The last major objective of the Antarctic explorers, once the Pole had been reached, was the crossing of the Antarctic continent. Shackleton set out to attempt this in 1914, but never succeeded. Another forty years were to pass before Dr. V. E. Fuchs successfully made the journey with his Sno-cats in 1957–58.

We have already mentioned some of the animals that are to be seen in the Antarctic, the most characteristic being the penguin. The Emperor penguin lays its eggs in the depth of the winter, and hatches the egg by holding it on its feet up against a bare patch of skin on its breast. It is the male bird who does all the incubating, standing on the ice, for the mother, as soon as she has laid her eggs, moves out across the ice to open water. The father is left alone to look after the egg for the sixty-day incubating period, but during this time he has no food at all, and all this in climatic conditions in which a man's skin would freeze in ninety seconds.

Another common bird is the skua, a large gull which preys upon the penguins eggs and chicks. He does not show the friendliness of the penguin, and becomes extremely angry if man intrudes upon his nesting grounds. Snow-white petrels are sometimes seen over the coast.

Before the Second World War there were still large numbers of blue fin and hump-backed whales in the waters of the Antarctic, but stocks have now been seriously depleted as a result of the modern methods of whaling and conservationists are seeking an international agreement on the limitation of permitted catches. The whales live chiefly on plankton, which is plentiful in the southern ocean in the summer. Some varieties of seal are still numerous, though the valuable fur seals have been almost exterminated. There are great numbers of crab-eater seals to be found in the pack-ice, and Weddell seals on the coast. Inland, there is virtually no animal life at all.

Antarctica, contrary to common belief, is neither silent nor altogether white. The blizzards provide plenty of shrieking and howling, and the ice fields crack and groan. The ice itself may be blue, not white, and so may the sky, though it is often a mass of fiery reds and yellows or during the winter nights, streaked by the curtain of shimmering colours which is called the *Aurora Australis*. It is certainly a very cold continent. During a warm summer day at the McMurdo Sound the temperature would still only be about −4 deg. C., while during the winter over 45 deg. C. of frost is not uncommon in Ross Island, and some of the members of Scott's last expedition experienced as much as 60 deg. C. of frost.

For men trying to live in the Antarctic, the blizzards are perhaps the most dangerous of the many threats to existence if only because of their unpredictability. At certain places in the Antarctic winds of hurricane force can spring up in a matter of moments. The driving drift snow they carry with them becomes so dense that it is impossible to see more than an arm's length in front of you, and is so fine that it drifts into everything. One particularly bad place was Sir Douglas Mawson's Adelie Land base of 1912–15, where he recorded an average wind velocity of 80 k.p.h. (50 m.p.h.); sometimes there were gusts of 320 k.p.h. (200 m.p.h.). Precipitation of water vapour in the form of rain is very rare, and the snow precipitation is surprisingly low; the estimated average fall of snow for one year on the Ross Ice Shelf is 33m (13 in).

At McMurdo Sound the sun shines for the whole twenty-four hours from the end of September to the end of February. After this, it begins to sink below the horizon for a longer and longer period each day until by mid-April it never appears at all and only gives a slight glow to the horizon at midday.

North America

CANADA
Nation in Commonwealth
Area: 9,976,000 sq. km/3,852,000 sq. miles
Population: 22,100,000   Capital: Ottawa
Flag: Red maple leaf on white ground flanked by vertical red bars

Canada is a country with very similar problems to the United States. It has a predominantly immigrant population settled over a vast area coming from very different backgrounds and with varying experience and education. Both countries have been faced with the task of forging a nation from widely-differing elements and the building up of a thriving and united community. Canada, although far larger in land area, has a population which is only a small fraction of that of America and compared with the United States is an almost undeveloped country. This does not mean that Canada is backward in any way, but that at the present moment with a population of over twenty-two millions scattered over such a vast area the nation lacks both the need and the people to exploit her potential wealth to the full. Her industries are highly developed and efficient and she has a thriving farming and fishing industry on an enormous scale, but she has been a nation for a far shorter time than the USA. It is only a little over a hundred years since the first Federation was set up, covering only a

An observation car on one of the Canadian Pacific trains. The domed roof gives an uninterrupted view of the landscape

An Eskimo drying skins which will be traded for such necessities as sugar, flour, tinned meats and oil

An aerial view of the mountains of Baffin Land, an island off Labrador, mainly inhabited by Eskimos

A young Eskimo boy of the Canadian far north. Although the Eskimo people are being influenced by the spread of Western styles of living, they still follow many of their old ways, which enable them to survive in their inhospitable climate

small fraction of the land that Canada covers today, and her economic, industrial and social problems are, generally, far simpler than those facing the United States. Agriculture, fishing and timber are the main products of Canada while the mining and processing of minerals and oil is of increasing importance. However, the United States with her advanced mechanical development is more important as a producer of finished goods from her own resources and imported materials, for a large proportion of which she depends on Canada.

Another of Canada's problems is the control of a huge area of, at present, unproductive polar regions. This is an area requiring special treatment to develop its potential. Canada shares with Russia and Denmark the responsibility for the wellbeing of the Eskimo inhabitants of the polar area, who have only very recently begun to develop beyond a fairly primitive state. If we look at a map of the whole of North America it is clear that the centre of activity and wealth for both countries is the land around the Great Lakes which lie in the middle of the continent. It is there that the main industrial centres are and there that raw material come from the mines and farms of both countries to be processed and transported to all parts of the continent and the world, and to supply both countries with the high standard of living for which both are famous and which continues to attract immigrants from all parts of the rest of the world.

Canada is a country of immense and striking geographical contrasts. It stretches from the Great Lakes on the boundary with the United States in the South to the North Pole. After the USSR it is the largest land area in a single confederation in the world. If we look at a map the areas of different land formations are very obvious. First we can see the huge mountain ranges running from south to north down the west side of the country. These are clearly an extension of the Rocky Mountains which dominate the same part of the USA. Although the mountains are less high than those of the USA they form a very definite change from the region in the centre of Canada which is a continuation into Ontario of the great Mid-West plain of the USA. To the east there is the region around the Great Lakes where, as in America, the distribution of the population is affected by the availability of cheap transport and a fertile hinterland. North of the Great Lakes is the area known as the Canadian Shield, a flat and virtually uninhabited area with many lakes and swamps now used mainly for growing timber and farther north as hunting and trapping grounds. To the far north are the arctic lands. These, north of the Arctic Circle, are known as the Northwest Territories and are mainly the home of the Eskimos.

These contrasts in geographical conditions naturally provide contrasts in the life of the Canadians who live and work in the country. The most heavily populated area is the south and east where the land is fertile and comparatively easy to farm, where there are rich mineral deposits and where there is easy access to the sea and to the central plains via the St. Lawrence Seaway and the Great Lakes. Farming is the most important occupation in Canada. It is claimed by the Canadian government that farming should be classed as an industry, so mechanized are the machines and methods used. One worker on a Canadian farm can now produce, on average, enough food for thirty-three people. Since there are still some small and unproductive farms this means that on some of the large prairie farms far more than this is produced by a single man.

In 1967 Canada celebrated its centenary as a nation and it provides a useful point at which to compare the development made by Canadians in their farming methods. In the 1970's nearly five times as much land is cultivated as in 1867, covering a total area of about 68·5 million hectares (170 million acres). It is also important to remember that in 1867 Canada was still in a fairly primitive stage of development compared to its situation today. Over 80 per cent of the population lived on agricultural land and the towns were very small; many of them were isolated and cut off from the rest of the country for long periods of the year.

Canada was originally discovered by John Cabot in 1497 and settlement began in the second half of the sixteenth century. Unlike the United States most settlement was made for trade, especially in furs, and the famous Hudson's Bay Company was established in the early years to act as a major trading company. One of the most important factors in the development of Canada was the existence of immigrants and representatives of both England and France at a time when England and France were at war in Europe. Continuous clashes between the two nationalities still present problems of language and precedent in the unified country where both French and English are official languages. Immigrants from other parts of the world are heavily outnumbered by the immigrants of French and British descent. There are about nine million Canadians of English descent and six million French while other nationalities make up a further seven million in a total population of twenty-two million. While Canada has successfully assimilated these elements into a single nationality, Quebec, the main French-speaking province, still holds out for the French links in a modern Canada and perhaps prevents the greater assimilation that has been achieved in the USA.

In addition to the immigrants in Canada there are the original inhabitants who lived there before the European colonization. All over the southern part of Canada there were Indian settlements which were gradually pushed back by the immigrants towards the western mountains. In the eighteenth century an agreement was made between the English settlers and the Indians to assure them a section of land as permanent hunting grounds in recompense for the land that had been occupied by the new settlements. The Indians are now being carefully integrated into the life of Canada and many work in public life and the professions. At the same time an attempt is being made to retain the Indian culture which has only recently been overlaid by more modern ways of life, and Indian art and crafts are carefully preserved. A similar problem of integration was posed by the Eskimos. Over 13,000 Eskimos live in the northern parts of Canada and until this century they lived in conditions that had not changed for hundreds of years. As with the Indians the problems of modern life were considerable, for the Eskimos had no resistance to European diseases and were in constant danger of exploitation by the traders who visited them. A careful programme of help and modernization has been carried out by the Canadian government in an attempt to prevent the hardships that the Eskimos suffered in the long winters when food supplies were very scarce and death and disease were constant threats. Hunting and fishing is still the major occupation of the Eskimos and an increasing number of projects are under way to improve conditions and exploit the potential of this relatively unknown land. The Eskimos still live a very different life from most Canadians. Although their traditional igloos are disappearing the sledge and fur clothes are still common means of travel and dress, and the Eskimo's language is retained in many areas. Like the Indians many Eskimos move down to the big cities to get jobs and live a more modern life with the rest of the population.

Three-quarters of the cultivated land in Canada is in the prairie land of Western Canada. As in the United States this is mainly used for grain and livestock and some dairy produce. This produce is of vital importance in Canada's exports. All farm produce makes up 25 per cent of Canada's total export and of this more than two-thirds is grain and grain products. Grain is now being sent in vast quantities to Russia, China and all countries with large populations and small or unproductive farmlands. Canada also retains her traditional markets in the United States and Great Britain while expanding in these other fields. Sales of livestock and dairy produce are almost as important though not as exports. To help the farmers the government of Canada provides many services of research, advice and financial help. Work is also being done on reclamation, irrigation and farmland rehabilita-

tion. Many areas of central Canada suffer from droughts especially in Alberta where there are now about 220,000 hectares (550,000 acres) of irrigated land. Soil improvement is also very important to an agricultural community to increase the fertility of the ground and a great deal has been done especially in British Columbia. In order to speed the sales of farm produce there are Boards for each type of produce such as wheat and milk which are responsible for overseeing the pricing and distribution of the goods produced by the farmer and guaranteeing him a fixed minimum price for his stock. Farming, although widespread in central Canada, is also of great importance in the east. Along the strip of land down the coast there is intensive dairy and fruit cultivation and the farmers are also famous for the quality of their vegetables.

Another of Canada's important industries is fishing. It was the quantity and quality of the cod shoals off the east coast of Canada which first attracted settlers in Canada, and the first discoveries of the continent were almost certainly made by Norse fishermen following the fish across the north Atlantic. The fishermen of Newfoundland produce huge quantities of cod every year both for the home markets and for salting for export. One of the more unlikely markets for Newfoundland cod is the Mediterranean lands and especially southern France where it is in great demand as a meal for the fast day, Friday. In 1949 Canada held over 25 per cent of the world market for salt cod, which as a cheap, long-lasting food was in great demand especially in the years after the Second World War when food was still in short supply. However the improvement in conditions in the 1950's meant that the cod fisheries had a declining market for their goods which were being produced by methods virtually unchanged for 200 years. A development scheme was drawn up and put into operation so that the fishing industry is now one of the most efficient in the country and is still responsible for a large proportion of the country's exports.

The other major fishing industry is centred on the other side of the country, in British Columbia. If you look at the map you can see that the coastline of British Columbia is made up of a series of bays and rivers, conditions which are very favourable for the highly profitable salmon fishing. Of the total

A machine for sowing wheat
on a farm in Winnipeg

Transferring wheat from the
harvester to a truck

Grain storage elevators in the
wheatbelt of Canada

Vancouver, in British Columbia, is the main port in the west of Canada. It is a busy industrial town and a railway terminus

catch, some is sold fresh but the majority is smoked or canned. Other fishing is also carried on in Canada; lobster fishing takes place on the coast of Prince Edward Island and provides the local fishermen with a very valuable source of revenue. Freshwater fish is very important for consumption in Canada; the large numbers of inland lakes and rivers were an important source of food centuries ago when the first explorers landed and remain as useful today. Canada's natural resources are not depleted as in so many older countries with longer histories of continual settlement, and the fact that the population is so very small compared to the total land area available means that her resources will be more than adequate for many years to come.

Fishing is the second largest and most important of Canada's primary products but no less important is the major resource of her inland provinces – timber. When Canada was first discovered, one of the most noticeable features about the interior of the country was the fact that it was covered with a dense forest. This made settlement difficult but provided shelter and building materials as well as firewood for the early pioneers. In more recent times the value of timber has been appreciated more and has increased considerably, and timber is now among Canada's most valuable exports. One of the worries about timber is the replacement problem. Originally the forest was cleared for settlement and the woodmen were regarded as performing a service by making spaces and providing materials for building and agriculture; more recently it has been realized that a great deal of valuable timber has been lost in this way, and, unlike farming land, timber needs many years to replace itself. It was only as recently as fifty years ago that the danger of complete loss of the forest was fully realized and intensive replanting has been developed since then;

The iron and steel plant at Hamilton, south Ontario

this has now reached the stage at which Canada has an assured future supply of timber, for more trees than she cuts and uses are grown annually.

The extent of the industry can only be fully realized when we look at the trade figures and realize that in any one year Canada receives over £750 million from her exports of timber after she has fully satisfied the demands made on timber at home. The position of the woodcutter or 'lumber jack' has changed considerably. In the past working in the forests was a rough job undertaken in bad conditions – you had to work through the long, hard winter and spend the summer looking for another job or living on the winter's wages. This was because logging used to be a seasonal job. The logs were cut and prepared in the long cold winter when the ice on the ground and the rivers made handling them much easier; then when the thaws came in spring the logs would be floated down the rivers to sawmills with the rush of water from the recently thawed mountain snow. Now methods and conditions have been modernized. The men live in modern buildings and instead of the old diet of dry biscuits and salt cod they have proper meals; they have modern equipment to work with, trucks to travel in and the logs are now transported by safer

methods than on the old log boom. This was a large structure of wooden planks which enclosed the logs and on which the men travelled down river to see that no logs floated away and guide them to the sawmill.

Another major industry in Canada is the mining and processing of minerals. The country is the world's leading producer of several valuable minerals, among them nickel, asbestos, platinum metals and zinc. All these are of great importance both at home and as exports. She is also the second largest producer of cobalt and uranium. Cobalt is mainly mined around the Ontario shores of the Hudson's Bay and farther north the then more exciting discovery of gold was first made. Gold created a great deal of attention in Canada in the last years of the nineteenth century, when the famous Klondike rush started in the Yukon territory; this failed to produce the fabulous quantities originally prophesied but still produced a very large weight and opened up the hitherto unknown territory. So isolated was it that the authorities insisted that any men who went up to the Yukon to prospect for gold must take with them stores for at least two years before they were allowed to cross the border. The main developments in mining for minerals have taken place since the Second World War. Rapid advances in methods and equipment have made advances possible on an unprecedented scale. The development of the minerals industry has had a very important effect on the transport system of the country. In the nineteenth century the country was virtually without any efficient means of transport apart from the few bad tracks which could take horses and carts. The manufacturing industries needed more efficient means of transport to cut their costs and make access to the raw materials easier. The railway was the obvious answer to this need and the Intercolonial Railway and the Canadian Pacific developed their lines to meet the expanding needs of the developing iron and steel and gold mining industries. The Yukon rush in 1896 encouraged the spread of the railways westwards and northwards following the transcontinental link made by the Canadian Pacific in the 1860's to carry the trade for the British Columbia gold rush. The servicing of sites has also encouraged new railways like the Quebec-Labrador railway in the early 1950's. Air development was the obvious answer to transport problems in a country where distances are so vast, and ever since

the 1920's the area covered by air flights has increased, although the railways have retained their traffic because of the continual need to transport goods to and from industrial sites in bulk.

We have already mentioned one of the most important developments in North American transport in this century – the opening in 1959 of the St. Lawrence Seaway. This is a route made along the length of the great St. Lawrence River to allow ocean going ships to reach the great towns in the centre of America. If you look at the map you can see the length of the stretch of water, from the mouth of the river at Newfoundland to Fort William on the far side of Lake Superior, a distance of some 3,700 km (2,300 miles). A plan to produce this great waterway began at the end of the last century when a start was made on a canal system designed to take large boats. The major problem was finding space to fit locks to carry the ships round the many waterfalls on the river and, most important, around the Niagara Falls. The Welland Canal linking Lake Ontario to Lake Erie with a depth of 8m (27 ft) was finally completed in 1932. However, this was only the first stage of the project and final agreement was only reached in 1954 on

Indigenous forest park in Vancouver

The St Lawrence Bridge, Quebec

The wooded Shield country, stretching to Hudson's Bay

the shape of the seaway. Like the other developments in Canadian transport the main reason for building the seaway was to help the development of Canadian industry. There were several important advantages. First the seaway provided the simplest means of transporting ore from the Labrador ore mines to the great steel factories in the Mid-West on the shores of the Great Lakes. There was a further gain in power and resources development in the construction of hydro-electric stations. The seaway also provided a means to get the grain produced in the prairie states quickly and cheaply to the coast and overseas. Iron ore, grain and coal were the main industries that benefited but timber movements were also considerable. These, together with various smaller commodities, make up a total of over fifty million tonnes of cargo with considerable savings to the producing and using industries. The seaway has obviously made a considerable difference to Canadian industry since it was opened and it will make a further contribution to life in Canada as industry develops and makes further use of the cheap transport facilities that it provides.

UNITED STATES
Republic
Area: 9,363,000 sq. km/3,615,000 sq. miles
Population: 211,400,000
Capital: Washington D.C.
Flag: Stars and Stripes
The United States of America covers a variety of climates and scenery and stretches from the Atlantic Ocean to the Pacific and from Canada to Mexico, and also includes Alaska and the Hawaiian Islands. The contrasts of temperature and surroundings in such a vast area are considerable. In a journey from east to west we would first cross the Appalachian mountains which are relatively low and extensively cultivated. We would then cross the huge plain of the Mid-West which takes hours to cross in a plane or train and days in a bus or car. It is completely flat for long distances until as we get further west there is a change, first to rougher prairie country, then to the sudden heights of the Rocky Mountains, rising to over 4,300m (14,000 ft). The land then slopes down towards the Pacific and here the climate is milder, especially in the Golden Valley of California where it is warm and gentle all the year round.

From north to south the contrasts are even greater. There are the Great Lakes which form the boundary with Canada for most of their length, and connecting waterways. These handle a large proportion of inland shipping, especially from the industrial complexes on the southern shores of the Lakes. Further south are the great flat farm growing belts and then the cotton growing belts of the deep south dominated by the great rivers, the Mississippi and the Missouri which flow out into the Gulf of Mexico with the semi desert of Texas to the west.

The population of this vast area is equally varied. Its discovery by Europe in 1492 when Columbus made his first landfall on the east coast began three centuries of colonization by several countries. As with most colonies at that time America was used as a dumping ground for transported criminals and as a haven for exiles. The first American communities included both these groups. The most numerous were the religious exiles from Europe in the early seventeenth century and it is from these groups that the oldest American families claim descent. The voyage of the *Mayflower* is the most familiar of these movements and it was these migrants who established the first settled communities. This constant flow of immigrants has dominated American life ever since. The years of highest immigration were those at the end of the last century and the beginning of this, and in all, since 1820 there have been 43 million immigrants. It is because of this vast number of people of all different nationalities that America is known as the 'melting pot' into which they have all been 'poured'. It is surprising for the visitor to America to see how far all these differences have become submerged in a single nation. One can still see traces of the older nationalities in surnames and in areas in the big towns, especially in the ports where immigrants first land, which are almost completely inhabited by single nationality groups. New York, for instance, has German, Polish and Chinese quarters, where food and clothing shops sell goods for one nationality. There are still about half a million descendants of the original inhabitants of the United States – the American Indians, and half of them still live on land specially set aside for them called reservations, where their old tribal life is preserved. The Black Americans were originally forcibly brought from Africa as slaves to work on

North America

ARCTIC OCEAN

BEAUFORT SEA

BAFFIN BAY

ELLESMERE ISLAND

QUEEN ELIZABETH ISLANDS

DISTRICT OF FRANKLIN

Brooks Range

Mt McKinley 20320 ▲

Alaska Range

ALASKA

U.S.A.

Fairbanks

Anchorage

NG STRAIT

SKA NSULA

Yukon

Dawson

YUKON

Whitehorse

Juneau

VICTORIA ISLAND

Great Bear Lake

Mackenzie

DISTRICT OF MACKENZIE

Liard

DISTRICT OF KEEWATIN

Gt.Slave Lake

COAST RANGE

BRITISH COLUMBIA

Peace

Lake Athabasca

C A N A D A

HUDSON BAY

BAFFIN ISLAND

LABRADOR

Churchill

NEWFOUNDLAND

St John's

Fraser

Mt Robson 12972 ▲

R O C K Y

ALBERTA

SASKATCHEWAN

Edmonton

Saskatchewan

MANITOBA

QUEBEC

Laurentian Highlands

GRAND BANKS

VANCOUVER ISLAND

Victoria

Vancouver

Seattle

WASHINGTON

Columbia

Regina

Lake Winnipeg

Winnipeg

ONTARIO

Quebec

NEW BRUNSWICK

Prince Edward

NOVA SCOTIA

Halifax

PACIFIC OCEAN

Cascade Ra.

OREGON

M O U N T A I N S

MONTANA

IDAHO

Snake

N.DAKOTA

S.DAKOTA

MINNESOTA

WISCONSIN

Lake Superior

Lake Huron

Montreal

Ottawa

St Lawrence

MAINE

NEW YORK

Toronto

L.Ontario

Buffalo

L.Erie

Niagara Falls

Mountains

Boston

ATLANTIC OCEAN

CALIFORNIA

Sierra Nevada

NEVADA

Gt Salt Lake

Salt Lake City

UTAH

WYOMING

U N I T E D

Platte

NEBRASKA

Minneapolis

Milwaukee

MICHIGAN

Lake Michigan

Detroit

Chicago

Cleveland

OHIO

INDIANA

Philadelphia

Pittsburg

PENNSYLVANIA

Long Island

New York

San Francisco

Mt Witney 14495 ▲

Death Valley

Grand Canyon

Colorado Plateau

Colorado

COLORADO

Denver

S T A T E S

Arkansas

KANSAS

ILLINOIS

Indianapolis

St Louis

MISSOURI

Ohio

KENTUCKY

Baltimore

Washington

VIRGINIA

Los Angeles

San Diego

ARIZONA

NEW MEXICO

Santa Fé

Oklahoma City

OKLAHOMA

Red

Memphis

TENNESSEE

Tennessee

Appalachian

N.CAROLINA

S.CAROLINA

MEXICO

Western Sierra Madre

Rio Grande

Conchos

Dallas

TEXAS

Houston

San Antonio

ARKANSAS

Mississippi

LOUISIANA

MISSISSIPPI

ALABAMA

GEORGIA

Atlanta

New Orleans

FLORIDA

Cape Canaveral

LOWER CALIFORNIA

Monterrey

León

Eastern Sierra Madre

GULF OF MEXICO

Mérida

Miami

BAHAMA IS.

Guadalajara

Santiago

México

Popocatepetl 17887 ▲

Southern Sierra Madre

Isthmus of Tehuantepec

YUCATAN

CUBA

JAMAICA

HAITI

DOMINICAN REPUBLIC

PUERTO RICO

CARIBBEAN SEA

CENTRAL AMERICA

SOUTH AMERICA

1	VERMONT
2	NEW HAMPSHIRE
3	MASSACHUSETTS
4	RHODE ISLAND
5	CONNECTICUT
6	NEW JERSEY
7	DELAWARE
8	MARYLAND
9	WEST VIRGINIA

0   500   1000   1500   2000 miles

0   1000   2000   3000 kilometres

the cotton plantations. Many of them have moved north to the industrial cities but the social position of the Blacks has given rise to much violence where social and civil disabilities exist. The total population has grown from 4 million in 1790 to over 200 million today but the growth is increasingly centred in specific points where the climate is best or opportunities are greatest. Thus the State of California has the highest population and New York the second highest while the farming communities are growing far less swiftly.

Some of the biggest cities are very well known. New York is probably the most famous; the main east coast port, it was the landing place for most immigrants from Europe and handles a third of all American trade. Its skyline displays some of the tallest buildings in the world – skyscrapers – and its crowded piers are familiar to many people as their first sight of America when they arrive by ship from Europe. The population of New York is over ten million which makes it the largest city in the United States while millions more come from suburban districts to work in the city. Like most large cities all these people create great traffic problems which New York has tried to solve by building six-lane highways around the city to carry the vast numbers of cars which are driven into the city every morning. The second largest city in America is Los Angeles, in California. Very close to it in population is Chicago, built along the banks of Lake Michigan in Illinois, which acts as a centre for the central plains of America. If you look at a map of America you can see how many of the major roads and railways pass through Chicago. Washington D.C., the capital of the USA is only the ninth largest town with a population of three-quarters of a million. It was one of the first towns to be planned as a capital city, and was laid out by a Frenchman called Pierre L'Enfant in the late eighteenth century.

Nearly two-thirds of the population live in towns and suburbs, which means that American life is mainly organized for people living in large communities. More than in any other country in the world, life in America is mechanized and simplified

One of the most famous views in the world, seen from the air. Manhattan is an island and was the original site of the first Dutch settlement in America

so that people have as much time as possible for activities apart from domestic chores.

However, there are still some very remote areas of America which are unaffected by modernization. The higher ranges of the Appalachian Mountains still contain people living in very primitive conditions and some religious sects such as the Amish people retain nineteenth century dress and habits from choice, and even refuse to own or ride in cars. To the rest of the world America seems a very rich country and in comparison with many other places it is very rich. One of the most obvious reasons for its wealth is the vast quantities of natural resources which the country contains. But resources alone do not make a country rich. In America the resources are accessible to the population by sea and river and good transport to the cities is easy and cheap. The great rivers of the USA such as the Mississippi, the Ohio, the Hudson and the Colorado flow through fertile valleys and provide fresh water for consumption and irrigation. This water made farming easier in the early pioneering days and more recently has made the development of large industrial sites possible. These rivers still provide over 50 per cent of water used for the cities and for irrigation and about 90 per cent of industrial fresh water. As in all industrialized countries there is an increasing fear of water shortages and the government is trying to

find a successful method of removing the salt from sea water and making it fit for consumption so as to increase available supplies of water. Frequently in the USA if there is a long dry summer the large cities are faced with serious water shortages and the people are warned to use water as sparingly as possible to prevent its waste.

Two hundred million hectares (nearly 500 million acres) of the USA is used as commercial forest land but altogether a third of the entire surface of the country is set aside as 'forest land'. Much of this land is used as parks and nature reserves where the people from the towns can spend their holidays and wildlife can be protected from the dangers of modern life. The annual growth of forest timber is only about one-sixth of the amount removed. In the west the forest lands are also used as grazing grounds for cattle and support more than three and a half million animals.

The mineral resources of the United States are another source of considerable wealth. Although some basic supplies have to be imported, more than seventy million tonnes of iron are produced every year for American manufacturing industries. Its uses are so many that it is utilized in over 200,000 different products of American industry and plays a very important part in the lives of all Americans. Most of the iron ore is mined in the north, over

Bryce Canyon in Utah, U.S.A. is a fantastic land of sandstone, carved by rain, frost, wind and sun into strange and beautifully coloured shapes

The arid Arizona desert produces these giant cacti

The Grand Canyon of the river Colorado, and the most spectacular canyon in the world, in some places 1.5 km deep

Florida, in the south east of the United States, has a tropical climate

Old Faithful, a hot water geyser in Yellowstone National Park, gives its spectacular display regularly every hour

three-quarters from the region around Lake Superior. Because the demand for ore is almost unlimited almost all the high grade ore has been used already; however there are still vast deposits of lower grade ore which need a more complex process to reduce them to iron and steel, though there is enough to last for several hundred years before the ore is completely worked out. The second major mineral produced in America is coal and although the part coal plays in industrial and domestic life is decreasing it is still of great importance, especially for domestic electricity. With modern methods of mining, the problems of obtaining the coal have been lessened considerably in America as elsewhere and the mining areas of the north are slowly losing their former depressing appearance. As industry expands more uses for coal are being discovered; it is used widely in the newer synthetics and chemical industries especially for the production of plastics so its position as a vital raw material is assured for some time.

The production of oil in the United States is especially high in the south and has been a source of wealth to many people who discovered oil deposits on land which they thought was useless. The vast desert areas of Texas are especially rich in deposits and the country as a whole has so much untapped oil that they are able to meet all the needs of the country in spite of its size and the many uses to which oil can be put. In the early 1970's the US produced nearly 3·5 billion barrels of crude petroleum per year. The processing and selling of oil, petrol and the by-products of refining oil is one of the biggest industries in the States. The important part that oil plays in American life is obvious in every town. The long distances travelled and the size of American cars means that huge quantities of petrol or gasoline are consumed every day in cars alone apart from other industrial and domestic use. Since 1957 the government has been experimenting in the production of oil from new sources since with such a vital commodity it would be unwise to depend on a single source. It was discovered that petrol could be obtained from a rock called gilsonite by means of heavy washing and then careful refining. This source of supply is considered to be a reliable one for many years. Gas, another source of power, supplies nearly 33 per cent of the nation's needs. Natural gas is carried in pipelines to towns and cities and is in use in many parts of the country. Other minerals that are produced in America include zinc, copper, silver and phosphate rock although these are all mined in considerably smaller quantities than iron ore, coal and oil.

If we look carefully at the map we can see how the industries use all these raw materials; all the towns of the north are large and centred on industry. They are placed on good transport routes which make it easier for the finished object to be transported from the factory where it is made to the person wanting to buy it or to the wholesaler who will distribute it to the customer. If you look at Detroit, the fifth largest town in the United States with a population of over one and a half million people you can see that it has all the advantages a large industrial city needs. It has access by water to the sea either up the St. Lawrence seaway through Canada or across Lake Erie and the Erie Canal to New York and the east coast. It is on the main east-west railway line which keeps contact with Chicago and the far west and it has road routes radiating from it out to all sections of the country. Detroit is most famous as the centre of a vast car industry employing thousands of people; the industry, almost more than any other, is dependent on good communications and a constant supply of raw materials which, in this case, come from Lake Superior by water; coal comes from the mining district around Pittsburgh by rail and truck. The big cities of the north with their large populations means that there are always plenty of people to work in the factories and to buy the goods when they are finished. Distances are so great in the United States – it is about as far from New York to California as it is from London to the Sudan – that transport presents problems. There is a network of railways, but these are less used by passengers than they used to be. Long-distance buses travel all over the States and internal airlines run flights rather on the same lines as the buses, with most small towns having an airport and people getting on and off informally, paying their fares to the stewardess when they are on board. Above all America relies on the motor car for transport. Very many families have two cars, one to take the husband into the nearest town to work and the other for the wife to use, whether it is to travel to her own job, to take the children to school or merely to go shopping. America did not grow up, as Europe did, from a series of small towns and villages connected by a network of minor roads, and often people live quite a long distance from a shopping centre and find it absolutely essential to have a car in order to bring home the things they buy. Most shops and stores do not have a delivery service and a lot of shopping is done by mail order.

This means that the motor car industry, centred in Detroit, is very important, particularly as Americans like to change their cars more frequently than do Europeans. Since the oil crisis in 1974 American cars have been, on the whole, growing smaller and more like European cars. In all factories automation is more general than in England and sophisticated machinery can take the place of large numbers of manual workers and turn out more goods in a shorter time. Computerization is widespread and increasing. Standards of living in the States are high, particularly in the north-east and the west coast, but there are still extremes of poverty in some of the backward areas of the south and in remote mountain places.

Schooling in America is compulsory from the age of 6 and the schools are often one of the centres of life in small towns, providing a common interest for all the townspeople whose children are taught there, as well as being a centre for community activities.

America has many beautiful and varied National Parks, offering every kind of sport and interest and camping and caravanning are popular.

Local government in America is run by elected representatives of the people and the 'Town Meeting' – a gathering of every interested citizen – can query decisions made by the administration and often reverse unpopular decisions.

One of the most important industries in America is farming. Half the total land area of the United States is farmland, half of which is used for growing crops and half for pasture for animals. Farming, like other occupations in America, is becoming more mechanized. In 1930 one man working on the farm produced enough food for ten people; now that one man can produce enough for thirty-three people. The main reason for this is the increase in farm machinery that makes sowing and harvesting of crops and the care of cattle much easier. The big combine harvester can cut a field and process the corn far more efficiently than by older methods and with the vast area under cultivation these methods are necessary. American farmers now use about one million combine-harvesters and over five million tractors. This sounds a very large amount of machinery but, since there are three and a half

A rich farming area in the San Joaquin Valley, California

A farm in a semi-desert region of the American West. By irrigation and careful planting, many millions of acres of this kind of land has been made productive

million farms in the country, when it is all divided up it is not very much. Of course some of the farms are just small family farms in which only the members of the family work to produce enough to make a livelihood for themselves, but although the average size of a farm is 130 hectares (330 acres) there are many especially in the farming state of Iowa in the Mid-West which are very much bigger and employ many men farming thousands of acres. So much corn is produced that the excess is sent abroad after all the needs of America have been met. The land available for farming has been increased by reclamation. This is mainly done by irrigating land which had become desert because it was so dry.

One of the major reasons for desert in America was the farming methods used when the land was first settled. The soil was very rich but the climate was so harsh that there was a constant danger of erosion or carrying away of the soil. When the land was farmed continually without any means used to prevent soil washing away in heavy rain or drying out in the dry season, fertile land quickly became unusable. In the early years of settlement the pioneers were so anxious to make their land pay that they did not take precautions to keep the land in good condition. The trees that sheltered the soil were chopped down to provide more growing land

and no fertilizers or fallow seasons were used. The government considered reclamation of this 'dust bowl' land as it was called so important that it set up a special department to deal with it and to reclaim land for farming by means of careful irrigation and planting. Millions of hectares have been reclaimed in this way and are now used for crop growing and pasture. There are well over a hundred million animals of all kinds on American farms and of these fifty million are cattle.

The great ranches of the West generally have many thousands of cattle which are still rounded up by cowboys for branding and slaughtering at long intervals. Chicago is a centre of some of the largest cattle markets in the world and the stock sheds stretch for several acres. The freezing of meat has revolutionized farming methods and freezing plants are widespread, animals being slaughtered and frozen in prime condition. Fishing is an important occupation. A very high proportion of fish is processed and frozen for transport to the big cities. Only half of the fish caught is used for human consumption, the rest goes to animal food and industrial use. Fish oil is also an important by-product for both industrial use and export.

Although the general picture of America is of a rich and well-fed country where there is plenty of food and space for everyone, like all countries it

A special attachment of the tractor cultivates between the rows of sweet corn on this Illinois farm

A herd of dairy cattle on a farm in Michigan

Mechanical rice harvesting in the Mississippi delta

has problems of poverty and disease. There are many districts in the large towns where living conditions are bad and overcrowded and where schools and hospitals can do little to educate or cure the people because their home condition is too bad to allow them to benefit from teaching or medicine. There is a system of social security designed to help those in great need. Social insurance provides some form of security for the old, unemployed and disabled but it is not enough to cover the needs of a family in great need. Medicare, a national form of medical insurance, now pays for a large amount of medical treatment which can otherwise prove cripplingly expensive, and there is a growing body of opinion in favour of the introduction of some system of state medical care.

The conditions in the slums of big cities have had the worst effect on certain minority groups in the population. Non-European immigrants and Blacks tend to live in special areas in the cities from which they cannot afford to move and where conditions are not always satisfactory. With bad housing conditions the people who live in these slums have often become desperate. There seems to be no escape from these conditions and violent riots have occurred, especially in the summer when the temperature in many American cities becomes very high and tempers are easily lost. Though it has often

Harvesting on the Great Plains, Colorado, with a team of combine harvesters

A bird's eye view of a new method of cultivating to increase crop yield on a farm in Washington State

been through violence that minority groups have made their demands heard, they are now increasingly represented in the government and in industry as well as in the academic world and the world of communications (television and radio).

As well as being a country of large resources America is also very beautiful. There are many natural wonders that Americans travel long distances to see. The Niagara Falls on the St. Lawrence seaway attract thousands of visitors – especially honeymooners – every year from both America and Canada to see the huge volume of water of one of the biggest waterfalls in the world. It is floodlit with many different coloured lights at night and there are lifts to carry the visitors up the front of the falls so that they can see the height of the drop. The National Parks are another attraction. There the original vegetation and wildlife of the country is preserved and visitors can drive for many miles through uninhabited land and see bears and wild buffalo roaming. In the Yellowstone National Park, one of the largest, there are hot geysers, the most famous of which, Old Faithful, shoots a jet of water steaming into the air every hour. The Grand Canyon, a natural valley carved by the water of the Colorado River, shows a series of rock formations

The United Nations Building in New York houses the
General Assembly and the Security Council

The great Horseshoe Falls of Niagara, separating the United States and Canada

through which the river valley has cut a steep gorge in many colours and is of great interest to geologists and holidaymakers alike.

America's history as a nation began in 1776 when the Declaration of Independence was adopted. Before then it had been a battleground for the colonial interests of the European countries and different parts of the country belonged to different countries. The Spaniards, the English and the French all had interests in America which originated in the discoveries of the sixteenth century and the settlements after 1600. The oldest building in the United States is in Santa Fe and is thought to have been built in 1619 by the Spaniards who held

New Mexico. When the English colonies declared their independence of the British Crown only thirteen states belonged to the Union. However since then the number of states has risen to fifty, of which the most recent are Alaska in the far north beyond Canada and Hawaii in the Pacific Ocean.

Government is organized on two levels, local or 'state' government by the individual states which make up the Union and central or 'federal' government by all the states in the Union working together. Federal government usually concerns matters which affect the whole country equally like foreign policy, wars, foreign trade with other countries and defence. The state governments deal

45

with matters of local importance like the police, marriage laws, education and local administration. The problems of this divided form of government are many. Where crime is concerned there are two forms of crime, state crime and federal crime, so if a criminal is found guilty in one state he might be liable for the death penalty while in another state he might only get five years in jail. Most states now have agreements which allow criminals who have escaped from jail or the police to be handed back to the state which is chasing them. Although it sounds confusing to have such a number of different sources of laws it is important to remember that each state is very large and that some are as big as single countries in Europe. Thus local laws apply to a very large area and encourage local interest by involving local people more than a government only for the country as a whole could do. Local government in provinces or states is the method used in both the United States and Canada to deal with the problems of government over the vast areas that these countries cover. Really it is the same type of government on a much larger scale as the system in England in which the local council has considerable powers of control. In both the United States and Canada, the local state government covers a huge area and has considerable powers but 'federal' or central government influence has been growing. Taxes are paid to both state and federal governments.

MEXICO
Republic
Area: 1,973,000 sq. km/762,000 sq. miles
Population: 54,300,000   Capital: Mexico City
Flag: Green, white, red vertical stripes with shield in centre
Linking South with North America is Mexico, a

The Library of Mexico University shows the use of ancient and traditional designs on a modern building

land which produced the Mayas, Aztecs and Toltecs, people as powerful and advanced in their civilizations as the Incas of Peru. The country is primarily agricultural although it is rich in minerals which have yet to be exploited; 60 per cent of the working population is engaged on the land. The most important crops are wheat and maize (corn), followed by beans. In recent years Mexico has become a tourist centre for people from North America because of its great natural beauties and the many fine archaeological sites, especially Chichen Itza, Teotihuacan, Mitla and Tula.

JAMAICA
Republic in Commonwealth
Area: 11,520 sq. km/4,410 sq. miles
Population: 2,000,000   Capital: Kingston
Flag: Green and black triangles divided by yellow diagonal cross

Jamaica is the third largest of the Caribbean Islands lying fairly close to the coast of the United States. It is 11,420 sq. km (4,410 sq. miles) in area with a central mountainous area and a ten-mile-wide flat coastal strip. It is in this coastal strip that most of the life of Jamaica centres since the main occupation is the production of agricultural produce for export. The climate is warm and damp and although Jamaica is part of the volcanic belt of central America there has been no serious disturbance since 1907. Rainfall can be very heavy in the inner parts of the island in the mountains where the temperature can also be very low, though the average is around 27 deg. C. and rainfalls about 200 cm (80 in) a year. The majority of the population of Jamaica are descended from the Africans brought over in the eighteenth century to work on the sugar plantations as slaves, and although there are other races, Chinese and East Indians, the descendants of the Africans and of marriages between slaves 'and the English sugar planters predominate. Jamaica still faces an employment problem which is reflected by the numbers of

The Panama Canal, which links the Pacific and the Atlantic Oceans

An open-air market in the West Indies

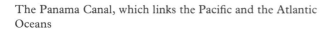

47

Jamaicans who emigrate every year in search of jobs.

The main sources of work in Jamaica are still the sugar plantations, which are as important today in the island economy as they were in the eighteenth century, and other agricultural products, some, like molasses a by-product of the sugar industry; the banana crop is another important employer of labour. Citrus fruits, cocoa, coffee and ginger are also important among Jamaica's export crops and the rum produced from the sugar cane is considered the best in the world. In 1973 sugar production was 342,000 tonnes. Beef cattle are also bred, including a local breed called the Jamaica Hope. However the most valuable of Jamaica's industries is no longer the product of the sugar plantations, and the island is now the largest producer in the world of the valuable mineral, bauxite. The industry is so valuable that the output of the mines covers about 70 per cent of Jamaica's total earnings of foreign currency. An Industrial Development Corporation provides financial incentives and encouragement to industries to settle in Jamaica. Already there are clothing, textiles, building materials factories, an important porcelain factory and a large refinery of oil for Esso. As a result of the amount of development in Jamaica there has naturally been a boom in building work. This has provided a ready market for goods produced by the factories and encouraged the development of more industrial production.

However, the most important asset of Jamaica is her natural beauty and climate. The ridge of the Blue Mountains towering up from the coastal plain has made the island an attraction ever since the fifteenth century. Columbus landed there in 1494 and the island was occupied by the Spanish and then by the British who captured it in 1655. Henry Morgan the notorious pirate lived there in the second half of the seventeenth century and during his lifetime Port Royal, then capital of Jamaica, was known as 'the wickedest city on earth'. It received its just reward, when, at the height of its notoriety as a centre of piracy in the Caribbean, it was engulfed by an earthquake in 1692. Lord Nelson also spent some time in Jamaica while

Left and right One of the main exports of the Caribbean is sugar cane, which is processed to give sugar, molasses, rum and also cattle feed

49

Gathering in the sugar cane
on carts drawn by pairs of
oxen

serving with the British Navy in the Caribbean and
Benebow and Rodney are also connected with Port
Royal. Kingston, the new capital, which was
established after the earthquake in Port Royal has
become a huge town with a quarter of the total
population living within its boundaries – about half
a million people. The other large towns are Mon-
tego Bay and Spanish Town. The majority of the
people still live in small towns and villages scattered
all round the island. With its historic past and its
natural beauty Jamaica is rapidly building up a
flourishing tourist trade.

Other important Commonwealth West Indian
islands in the Caribbean are Bahamas, Barbados
and Trinidad. In many ways they follow the same
patterns of life as Jamaica.

South America

BRAZIL
Republic
Area: 8,512,000 sq. km/3,286,000 sq. miles
Population: 101,700,000   Capital: Brasilia
Flag: Green with yellow diamond in centre containing blue sphere slashed with white band with stars

Brazil is the fifth largest country in the world, and it has the eighth largest population. Covering nearly one half of the South American sub-continent, Brazil has a larger land surface than Australia. From north to south it is 3,700 km (2,300 miles), and almost the same distance from east to west. A large part of the country is taken up by the basin of the mighty River Amazon, whose source is found among the Andes Mountains on the western side of the continent, while her mouth is 6,500 km (4,000 miles) away where the Equator crosses the coast on the Atlantic side. The river flows through a broad, flat plain which narrows gradually as it approaches the coast. Here, there is very heavy rainfall, some places receiving as much as 400 or 500 cm (150 or 200 in) per year, though the average fall is about 150 to 250 cm (60 to 100 in). The flat areas beside the rivers are often flooded. Everywhere there is thick, tropical forest, making it difficult to penetrate the territory, and the hot, damp climate is not pleasant to live in.

The La Plata basin in the southern part of Brazil is a much more hospitable place. Here the land surface is more varied, and there is less forest. The land is higher than in the Amazon basin – where most of the drained area is less than 240m (800 ft) above sea level – and the climate cooler.

The other two geographical areas are both formed of highland. To the north of the Amazon lie the Guyana Highlands, to the south and west of the Amazon, the Brazilian Highlands. The Guyana Highlands are mainly either hot, stony desert or forest-covered hills. Rainfall varies considerably from region to region. The hot summers are matched by cool winters. The Brazilian Highlands stand, on average, between 300 and 900m (1,000 and 3,000 ft) above sea level, though, towards the east, ranges of mountains rise from the tableland. The highest peak in Brazil is 2,787m (9,140 ft) high. Along the coast from Porto Alegre to Salvador the Great Escarpment falls sharply down towards the sea in parallel steps, each step separated by the trough of a valley. This makes communications between the coastal areas and the highlands difficult. A few rivers flow down the eastern slope of the escarpment to the sea, but the majority of them flow inland, either to join the River Parana which turns southwards to reach the sea as the River Plate, or flow into the Sao Francisco River, which travels northwards parallel with the coast for 2,900 km (1,800 miles) before it runs eastward into the Atlantic. The narrow coastal strip between the Great Escarpment and the sea is on average only 100 km (62 miles) wide and occupies only 7 per cent of Brazil's total area. Yet it is here that most of the great cities are to be found, and it is the home of 36 per cent of the Brazilian people.

To the outside world, Brazil is best-known as the greatest of coffee producing countries, and coffee occupies a very large place in the Brazilian economy. Coffee did not originate in Brazil. According to a well-established legend, it was first drunk in the Middle East. In the fifteenth century, a goatherd named Kaldi, who tended his animals on pasture that lay near a monastery, noticed that they became very lively when they ate some berries that grew near by. Kaldi told one of the monks about this, who decided that he would try the berries for himself. After trying various ways of preparing them, he decided that it was best to boil them, and the beverage that resulted helped to keep the monks awake during their night services. Though many people soon heard about the drink, it was some time before it began to be grown farther afield; by the early sixteenth century, however, Turkish and Dutch traders had taken seeds to their own countries. Coffee came to South America through the offices of a young French naval captain called de Clieu, who took it to Martinique, whence it passed eventually to the mainland. De Clieu's journey over the Atlantic was not without its difficulties, either for himself or for the coffee plant. 'Water was lacking to such an extent,' he said, 'that I was forced to share my scanty ration with my coffee plant upon which my highest hopes were founded and which was the source of my delight.'

Coffee eventually came to Brazil thanks to Sergeant Major Francisco de Melo Palheta. He is said to have been given the seeds in 1727 by the wife of the Governor of French Guiana, in violation of a law passed by the King of France, who wished to maintain his monopoly of the plant in the area. Palheta's seeds became a plantation of more than a thousand bushes in the Brazilian interior. By the end of the eighteenth century, coffee farms –

Blocks of modern flats and offices in Rio de Janeiro

A panoramic view of Rio de Janeiro, showing the magnificent harbour. The tall peak is the famous Sugar Loaf Mountain

Belo Horizonte, a new industrial city north of Rio de Janeiro

Terraces of slum houses in a shanty town on the outskirts of Rio de Janeiro. Such shanty towns spring up when people crowd into the city to look for work

A tree-top view of the dense Amazon jungle in Brazil

Vast areas of Brazil are covered by almost impenetrable rain forest like this

Fazendas – were a familiar sight in the provinces of Para, Bahia, Rio de Janeiro and Sao Paulo. The crop showed itself to be admirably suited to the climate and terrain of Brazil, and it flourished wherever it was grown.

Coffee plants are at first small and delicate, and require adequate and regular watering preferably in a tropical climate where the average temperature is between 18 deg. C. and 21 deg. C. It is important that there should be no heavy rains during the flowering season and no frost at any time. Coffee grows best in the shade, though the yield may be larger and easier to pick if there are no shade trees in the way. This kind of farming, however, tends to result in the land getting exhausted more rapidly. Eventually, of course, it will get exhausted anyway, and, in the early days, farmers used then to move to a new area, but today crop rotation and scientific treatment help to keep the soil well nourished.

When seeds are needed for planting, the largest fruit is selected from a parent bush of about seven or eight years, which is known for its high productivity. When it is thoroughly ripe, the pulp is removed by hand, taking care not to break the parchment-like covering. Coffee germinates in about six or seven weeks, but the seed will not produce a crop for from three to five years. A grown plant may be 2m (7 ft) high or 6m (20 ft) high. Its leaves are dark green and its branches long and flexible. Each bush may flower several times a year, its small white blossoms giving off a pleasant scent. The berries are at first dark green, but they change colour as they mature, passing from green to yellow and finally to a deep crimson.

The two beans of 'green' coffee inside each berry are well covered. The ripe berries are harvested any time between spring and autumn, and are usually spread out in a thin layer on the ground and turned over several times a day to expose them to the sun and wind that will dry them. Alternatively, they may be dried by machine. When this process has been completed, hulling machines remove the outer coverings, the beans are weighed and bagged and finally sent off to the nearest port for shipment.

As much as one half of the labour force of Brazil is engaged in the growing of coffee. The *fazendas* are complete self-contained communities for those who work on them: there are not only their houses, but also a school, a church, and land where fruit and vegetables may be grown and animals raised.

Modern buildings in Brasilia, the capital of Brazil

The centre is usually the owner's house, a large white building.

The new city of Brasilia was inaugurated as capital of Brazil in 1960. Formerly, Rio de Janeiro was the capital, but it was long felt that this great, overcrowded city, lying on the rich coastal belt in the south-east of the country, could never be seen to be representative of the country as a whole, and that from an administrative point of view, it was far too distant from many parts of the country. Accordingly a site was chosen for an entirely new city to be built, high up in the Brazilian Highlands. In style it was to be entirely modern, a symbol of the unity and progressiveness of the Brazilian people. A competition was held in order to find the best design for the new city. The winning plan conceived the city as a bent bow and arrow or a cross in which the vertical piece was bent to follow the lines of the lake. The three powers, the Executive, the Supreme Court, and the Federal Congress were placed at the three corners of a triangle, while in front of the Congress was an immense rectangular esplanade along which the ministerial buildings were constructed. In another part, all the 'cultural' buildings – the museums, libraries and societies – are kept together in an area of parkland, and near by is the University City, the hospital and the observatory. These centres of interest – and there are others too: a hotel centre, a radio city, an area of fairs and circuses, a centre for sports, a municipal

square – are all placed along the arrow, as it were, with the Plaza of the Three Powers at the head of the arrow, the cultural and recreational centres where the bow and arrow intersect, and the railway station where the string of the bow would be. At either side of the intersection are the commercial areas. The residential areas are strung out along the curve of the bow, and arranged in the form of a number of self-contained communities; each community will eventually have its own school, shops, theatre and parking places. This makes it unnecessary for people to travel backwards and forwards across the city from shopping areas to entertainment areas to residential areas and helps to foster a sense of community living.

After coffee, Brazil's most important agricultural export is cocoa. Unlike coffee, this plant is native to the Americas, and it played an important part in the religious rituals of the Aztecs. According to Aztec mythology, the cocoa seed was a divine gift given to man by Quetzalcoatl, god of the air. The Aztecs believed that he was punished by the other gods for his pains, but humanity remembered his gift gratefully. The beans were used to prepare a drink called *choclatl* meaning 'warm drink'. They were first dried in the sun, then roasted in earthen pots and ground to powder between stones. The powder was mixed with spices and moulded into cakes, which were, in turn, pulverized and mixed with water. In the time before Cortes invaded Mexico, cocoa beans were used not only to make *chocolatl*, but also served as money. There is record of them being used, for example, to pay tribute to the Emperor, or to buy slaves.

Until the middle of the nineteenth century, cocoa continued to be used exclusively as a beverage. Attempts had been made to make bars of chocolate in which sugar was added to the cocoa, but the end product was too coarse and dry to be popular. Some manufacturers then discovered that by adding extra cocoa-butter to the mixture of cocoa and sugar, they could produce chocolate with a smooth, creamy texture, and from then on the demand for eating chocolate became ever greater. The cocoa tree is a native of the low-lying forests of the Amazon-Orinoco Basin, where it grows under the shade of the larger forest trees. The height of a fully-grown cocoa tree is generally about 7 to 10m (20 to 30 ft).

The leaves of the young cocoa plant are red or light green, but as the plant matures they gradually turn a dark green. The buds, flowers and fruit eventually appear on the older, leafless part of the tree. The fruit comes in the form of a pod, 15 to 25 cm (6 to 10 in) long, which contains thirty to forty seeds. The shape and texture of the pod – round or long, furrowed or smooth – varies according to the type of cocoa plant. One can expect to find the pods fully developed about five or six months after the time of flowering. The thick, woody exterior of the pod contains a pulp in which are embedded the seeds. When they have been extracted, these have to be fermented and dried.

Since the late 1960's great strides have been made in industry, notably steel and shipbuilding.

COLOMBIA
Republic
Area: 1,139,000 sq. km/440,000 sq. miles
Population: 23,200,000   Capital: Bogotá
Flag: Upper half broad yellow band with equal bands of blue and red below

To the north of Brazil are the three republics of Colombia, Ecuador and Venezuela. Colombia takes its name from Christopher Columbus who first sighted it in 1502. It was under Spanish rule until 1819 when it became independent as a result of a revolution led by Simon Bolivar, a South American patriot whose name is perpetuated in another republic, Bolivia. Colombia is mainly an agricultural country whose main crop is coffee. Livestock is reared on the endless grasslands (llanos) and hides are an important export. At one time gold was the most valuable mineral but its place has been taken by petroleum. Colombia also produces about 90 per cent of the world's emeralds and half the world's platinum.

Tin mine workings in Bolivia. Though other minerals are mined, tin is Bolivia's main export

Above left
Indian women of the high Andes spinning llama wool to make cloth. The 'bowler' hat is part of their national costume

Left
Bolivian Indian women preparing the land for planting potatoes. In the background is Lake Titicaca, the highest lake in the world

Above
Bolivian Indians ploughing the stony land with a wooden plough drawn by an ox

Right
Oil rigs in the Gulf of Maracaibo, Venezuela

The oil refinery at Curaçao, Venezuela

ECUADOR
Republic
Area: 455,000 sq. km/176,000 sq. miles
Population: 6,700,000   Capital: Quito
Flag: Yellow, blue, red horizontal bands with emblem in centre
Ecuador to the south-west of Colombia has much the same geography as this country to which it was linked until 1830; large areas have still to be mapped. It is mainly an agricultural country; coffee and bananas are important crops. Its most important product is petroleum. Another large producer of petroleum is Venezuela; there it is worked around the shores of Lake Maracaiba.

PERU
Republic
Area: 1,285,000 sq. km/496,000 sq. miles
Population: 14,100,000   Capital: Lima
Flag: Red, white and red vertical bands with national emblem in centre
Peru lies on the west coast of southern America, north of Chile. The coastline consists of the narrow strip of land to the west of the Andes which form a high ridge very close to the sea. Inland there is a fertile area well watered by rivers which flow down to the Amazon basin on the east and provide irrigation for agriculture. There are some areas of Peru which have rain only once every fifteen years and it is therefore very dependent on the rivers fed by the snow from the Andes.

Peru was first discovered and conquered by the Spaniards under Pizarro in the sixteenth century.

The country was inhabited by a race of people known to the Europeans as the 'Incas'. They had achieved a level of civilization which astonished the invading Spaniards. They lived in large towns and the centre of their civilization was the worship of the Sun God to whom they gave presents of quantities of gold which Peru then possessed in vast amounts. The gold, which was a decorative metal to the Incas who did not use money as a means of exchange, aroused the greed of the Spaniards who virtually obliterated the Inca civilization and plundered the gold-decorated temples and buildings of the cities. The Spanish colonization is still obvious in Peru; there are many buildings which are very reminiscent of Spanish building and the names of many of the inhabitants show their Spanish descent. The country had many other advantages, apart from gold, for the invaders. The land was fertile and well farmed and the towns although high up in the mountains were well built and well designed. The Spaniards erected their cities on the foundations laid by their Inca predecessors and many towns, such as the town of Cuzco, are still built on the same street plan as the old Inca cities.

There are many Peruvian legends about the origins of the Incas, the 'Children of the Sun'. One claimed that the original Incas were descended from the son and daughter of the Sun God himself and were set down in the mountains to wander until they found a site for their capital. When they reached the valley of Cuzco, with its broad fertile plain and protecting hills they founded their city and the Inca Empire there. There was built the most important building in the Empire, the 'coricancha', the temple of the Sun. The building was completely covered with beaten gold ornaments including a great round plaque with the face of the Sun God on it, specially placed to catch the rays of the morning sun. The Golden Garden of the Sun was also in Cuzco. It was made entirely out of gold with trees, flowers, animals and birds all made of pure gold. There were many festivals all year, but the most important was the Solemn Feast of the Sun; to attend this feast people travelled from all over the Empire to watch the sun rise in the Sacred

Machu-Picchu, the ancient capital of the Incas of Peru

60

Farming under the towering Peruvian Andes

Square of Cuzco. When the sun appeared the chief or *supa* Inca poured a libation to his father the Sun and asked for his blessing. Offerings were then made in the Temple of the Sun and there were nine days of celebrations.

The Incas ruled their empire well. The land was divided into three groups; one for the Sun and the upkeep of the priests of the Sun God; one to be worked for the Inca – the nobility of the empire; the remaining third was for the *ayllus* or the tribal groups of the people who were the workers of the empire. The Incas had a strict quota of work – only men between the ages of twenty-five and fifty were allowed to work in the fields. This age group was also liable for military duties; women and children worked at home. There were no money taxes paid but a certain amount of the annual produce was given to the priests and the Inca, and a fixed labour service was due to the Inca to work the lands set aside for the priests and the Inca. People with special skills were exempt from many of the services and concentrated on their particular skill such as road making or construction of buildings. While work was done for the Inca, food, clothing, and materials were provided but the work-service was only exacted at certain periods in the year. There were also several days a year which were fixed as holidays for the whole country; all the people took part in the festivities and were exempt from all kinds of labour on these days.

The country was also united by a common language, *Quechua*, which was the official language for all the provinces and colonies of the Inca Empire. The Empire covered a very wide area of land and, as in most countries, there was a problem of transferring messages from one part of the country to the other. The Incas developed a remarkable system of runners who ran at a high speed along the many roads of the Empire.

The Inca craftsmen were magnificent builders. If you look at a picture of an Inca building you can see that they constructed massive fortifications without the use of any mortar. They carved great blocks of stone and slid them together so well that many are still as strong to day as when they were first built. One of the most remarkable examples of Inca building is the fortress of Machu Picchu. This mountain fortress was only discovered in 1911 by an American who was an expert in Incan history. It stands high up in the mountains over the valley of Cuzco and it is thought that it was the refuge of the Virgins of the Sun who fled from the marauding Spaniards when they overran the Inca empire. The towers and buildings of the city are still standing and the layout of the fort can be seen very clearly. In Cuzco itself there are still many reminders of the Incas. Often the stonework of the buildings was so strong that it was easier for the Spaniards to incorporate it into the walls of their houses than to raze it to the ground and build new foundations. An example of such a wall is the curved end wall of the great temple of the Sun God which was destroyed by the invaders; the wall remains as part of the end wall of the monastery which was established on the site of the temple and is a perfect example of the skill of the Inca craftsman.

Although the Incan empire vanished nearly four hundred years ago, it is still possible to find out a great deal about the lives that people lived. One reason for this is that many Inca settlements were deserted when the Spaniards came and, like Machu Picchu, only need excavating to discover many details of Inca life, because they were not disturbed by later inhabitants. All these remains of the old Incan Empire are being very carefully restored by the Peruvian government. They are an obvious attraction for tourists and the sites are being developed and large hotels are being built close to them to encourage visitors.

A herd of alpacas in the Andes. These animals are closely related to the llamas

The way of life of most Peruvians today is often very similar to that of their Inca ancestors. Their clothes and food are often unchanged; they live mainly on cereals with a little meat and at their feasts sing songs and dance dances which are at least as old as the Incas. The country is still mainly agricultural though fishing is important, and normally more fishmeal is produced than in any other country in the world; most of the people live in small communities which are very different from the busy modern towns like Lima, the capital, where there are tall flats and offices like those in large towns all over the world, and where the car and bus have supplanted the donkey which is still the commonest form of transport in the remoter country districts.

CHILE
Republic
Area: 757,000 sq. km/292,000 sq. miles
Population: 10,200,000   Capital: Santiago
Flag: White and red horizontal bands with white star on blue square at top left

Chile is one of the most curiously shaped countries in the world. It is nearly 4,800 km (3,000 miles) long but is, on average, no more than 160 km (100 miles) wide. On the map you can see that this long and uneven shape gives Chile as much as possible of the very narrow strip of low-lying land along the shore of the Pacific Ocean, as well as a narrow section of the Andes, the great ridge of volcanic mountains which dominates western South Ameri-

CENTRAL
AMERICA
(see inset)

South and Central America

VENEZUELA

Orinoco

Caracas

GUYANA

Georgetown

SURINAM

Paramaribo

FR. GUIANA

Cayenne

Bogotá

Magdalena

COLOMBIA

RIO
BRANCO

Branco

AMAPA

The mouths of
the Amazon

Quito

ECUADOR

Negro

Obidos

Belém

Putumayo

Amazon

Manaus

PARA

Fortaleza

Marañon

A M A Z O N A S

Juruá

Purus

ACRE

Madeira

Tapajós

Xingu

Araguaia

São Francisco

Recife

Huascarán
22 211

Ucayali

MONTANA

B R A Z I L

BAHIA

Lima

Madre de Dios

Guaporé

Tocantins

Campo

PERU

Cuzco

BOLIVIA

Plateau of

Brasilia

Salvador

Lake
Titicaca

Illampu
21276

Mato Grosso

Brazil

Arequipa

La Paz

Oruro

Santa Cruz

Plateaulands

MINAS GERAIS

Belo Horizonte

Sucre

PACIFIC

Paraguay

Highlands

São
Paulo

Paraná

SÃO PAULO

Brazilian

Rio de Janeiro

Llullaillaco
22 057

Pilcomayo

PARAGUAY

OCEAN

Tucumán

Asunción

Uruguay

RIO GRANDE
DO SUL

500 miles

1000

0

500

1000

1500 kilometres

Aconcagua
22 834

Córdoba

Paraná

Santa Fé

Rosario

URUGUAY

Pôrto Alegre

Valparaiso

Santiago

Buenos Aires

Montevideo

Concepción

Bahía Blanca

M E X I C O

Negro

CARIBBEAN

BELIZE

Belize

PATAGONIA

GUATEMALA

SEA

Chonos
Archipelago

Guatemala

HONDURAS

San Salvador

Tegucigalpa

EL
SALVADOR

NICARAGUA

Managua

COSTA
RICA

Straits of
Magellan

FALKLAND
ISLANDS
P. Stanley

S. José

Panama Canal

Tierra del Fuego

PANAMA

Cape
Horn

100 200 300 400 500 miles

0

250

500

750 kilometres

A roadway torn apart during an earthquake in Chile, a country wholly in the earthquake belt of South America. There are also many active volcanoes in the Chilean Andes

ca. The Andes contain some of the highest and the most active volcanoes in the world and seldom a year passes without some earth tremor or more disastrous eruption from the volcanoes. Of course the volcanoes mean that the land around the mountains can be very fertile and in central Chile there is some rich farming land, though the amount available for farming is small so that to work it productively is very difficult.

The area covered by Chile is larger than any European country except Russia, so that in spite of its small width, its length gives it a very varied climate. It contains both some of the driest desert and the wettest forest areas in the world. In parts of the Atacama desert rain has never been recorded, while the forested areas in the south have a rainfall of 570 cm (225 in) a year, higher than anywhere else outside the tropics. The central and most populous area of Chile however escapes both these extremes and has a temperate mediterranean climate

and rich agricultural land. Farming is on a very large scale and wheat, fruit and especially wines are produced in large quantities. Here also are the main cities of Chile; Santiago, the capital, has a population of four million, over a third of the entire population, while 130 km (80 miles) to the west is Valparaiso, the second largest city and chief port of Chile. Concepcion further south is the centre of a large manufacturing industry, concentrating on textiles, paper and electrical machinery.

The population of Chile is fairly mixed. Before settlement by the Spaniards in the sixteenth and seventeenth centuries Chile was inhabited by an Indian population belonging to three separate tribes; when the Spanish settlers came there was a great deal of inter-marriage with the Indians, and a mixed Spanish Indian race developed as well as the descendants of other European immigrants. One of the most interesting of these European settlers was a party of Welsh emigrants who settled

65

The Atacama Desert in northern Chile, a barren region, but rich in minerals

in southern Chile at the beginning of the nineteenth century; they continue to live in communities based on a Welsh village pattern and are bilingual in Welsh and Spanish.

Chile has developed a fairly high level of industrialization and now uses more fuel and power per head of population than any other South American country. This is the result of the very rich mineral deposits which have been discovered in Chile and worked both by the Spaniards and by the Chileans. The most important of the minerals today is copper which accounts for about two-thirds of the country's exports. Chilean deposits of copper have been estimated as about a third of the total world supply and, while these are very important, the region in northern Chile where they are mined also produces considerable quantities of iron ore, gold and silver. Another important mineral deposit in Chile is the nitrates mined in the desert which together with large deposits of guano on the coast provide vital fertilizers for farming. Before 1914 Chile had almost a monopoly in the production of nitrates and supplied two-thirds of the world's stock of fertilizers. However, with the developments of artificial fertilizers the industry is decreasing in importance and has been succeeded by iron ore as the second most important mineral mined in Chile. In 1945 oil was discovered and the industry is now completely self-supporting. Oil is no longer imported. There are also several minor industries, the most important of which is the newly developed cotton and woollen textile industry in Santiago.

Agriculture in Chile presents many problems. Most of it is done by small peasant farmers with a very low level of productivity. With its rich soil and temperate climate Chile could be self-supporting but at the moment has to import a great deal of food every year. Increased production on the farms is failing to keep up with the growing population and is presenting many problems. The first is one of education of the farmer in modern methods which will help him to improve and increase his crops. Production is at the same level as it was twenty years ago so there is obviously a great need for improvement. Land-holding is another important reform to provide land in sufficient areas so that it can be farmed economically, free from the heavy burdens of the old system of land tenure from the wealthy land owning class. In 1955, before the land reform introduced by President Allende, Chile contained many extremely large farms, of some 5,000 hectares (12,000 acres) or more, while 50,000 peasants had scarcely more than 1 hectare (2.5 acres) per family, but by early 1972 3,601 farms (covering some 7,000,000 hectares, or 18,000,000 acres) had been expropriated and 43,000 families resettled. Further efforts are being made to expand electrification to as many farms as possible and to establish

Vineyards in the central
region of Chile

Peaks and glaciers in the
Andes, a range stretching
along the entire Pacific coast
of South America

co-operatives to market the food produced on the farms.

One of Chile's greatest problems apart from agriculture is the condition of the population. Until very recently the majority of Chileans were illiterate; they lived on the land as tenants to land-owners and made little more than a subsistence living by farming rented land. This meant that any form of development was unable to establish itself and industry was weakened because of the absence of a market for manufactured goods. The changes are bound to be slow but already Chile is developing, education is free and compulsory and the new agricultural reforms and industrial developments seem to indicate that Chile will develop into a successfully modernized country. The areas of Chile which are not fit for industrial or agricultural development are being considered as possible tourist centres. The southern end of Chile running down to Tierra del Fuego on the southern tip of South America is a region made up of lakes and deep valleys of considerable beauty which it is hoped will attract the attention of visitors from North America.

ARGENTINA
Republic
Area: 2,777,000 sq. km/1,072,000 sq. miles
Population: 24,300,000
Capital: Buenos Aires
Flag: Blue, white, blue horizontal stripes with emblem in centre

The River Plate estuary was discovered in 1515 by the Spaniard Juan Diaz de Solis, and nineteen years later, Buenos Aires, the present capital of Argentina, was founded. The area did not develop rapidly as a colony, for Buenos Aires was abandoned and had to be refounded towards the end of the century. Argentina remained under Spanish rule until the beginning of the nineteenth century, when a six-year war of liberation under the leadership of General José de San Martin ended with the declaration of the country's independence in 1816. Today, it is an independent republic, though the signs of the long rule of the Spanish – the predominance of the Catholic religion, and the continued use of the Spanish language and literature – still survive.

Argentinian territory extends from the highlands of Bolivia in the north to the Tierra del Fuego, the southernmost tip of South America. To the east lies the Atlantic Ocean, and Uruguay, Paraguay and Brazil; to the west the Cordillera de los Andes, and Chile. The country is divided into areas of plateau, bounded by mountain and sea. In the north there are the thickly forested plains known as El Gran Chaco, while the central part of the country, down as far as the Rio Negro, is occupied by the treeless pampas, one of the chief cattle-raising areas in the world. In the southern, narrow part of the country are the higher plains of Patagonia, where the country is rougher and less productive and the climate far colder. The greatest of the mountain ranges are the eastern spurs of the Andes, but there are also the San Luis and Cordoba Ranges, jutting out from the Andes, in the province of Cordoba, while between Buenos Aires and Bahia Blanca there are the Tandil Hills and the Sierra Vantana.

There are more than 160 million hectares (400 million acres) of farm land in Argentina and about 60 per cent of this is used for pasture, divided into large farms wholly devoted to the raising of cattle and sheep. But the number of small farms in the country is increasing, and crops are also important, notably wheat, maize, rye, barley and oats, as well as sunflower seed, sugar and cotton. Argentina produces enough of the basic foodstuffs to be able to feed herself and still have enough to spare for a large export industry. The greater part of this production originates in the pampas. She is also a large producer of wine.

The biggest problem on the *estancia*, or cattle-farm, is keeping up the water supply. The rainy season is a short one, lasting only from December to January, while at other times of the year there may be serious droughts. So that there may be sufficient water for the cattle, wind-pumps are used to draw water up from wells.

The pampas, once covered with tough, wiry grass, has generally been planted by the farmers with grasses better-suited to grazing cattle. The cattle are cared for, as they rove over the miles of flat tableland, by cowboys known as *gauchos*, part-European, part-Indian people whose ability to handle horses is famed far beyond the boundaries of Argentina itself. These men keep cattle or sheep moving over the pastures so as to keep the grasslands in as good a condition as possible and to be sure that there will always be foodstuffs for the

A 'gaucho' or cowboy herding cattle into a stockade. Gauchos are of mixed Spanish and Indian descent

animals. They must also see that they are dipped regularly, and drive them to the railway or the river when it is time for them to be sold. At the same time there are a great number of horses to look after, for these men cover such great distances in a day that they may have to change horses four or five times before evening.

Very important natural resources that are being exploited more and more in Argentina are oil and natural gas. The country that has oil today is in a very advantageous position, for it does not have to go to the expense of buying from abroad a substance that is basic to much of modern commerce and industry – motor-cars and diesel engines, heating, and the increasingly wide range of petro-chemical and allied industries.

Europe

ICELAND
Republic
Area: 103,000 sq. km/39,800 sq. miles
Population: 210,000   Capital: Reykjavik
Flag: Blue with red cross bordered white

Iceland is an island, rather larger than Ireland, with a population of over 200,000 and lies on the very edge of the Arctic Circle. Many people know it as *the land of ice and fire*, for it is a country of contrasts and a difficult land to live in. In winter the snows cover the roads and the cultivated land, and, in the highlands, where there is always snow, glaciers creep down from the mountains. At the same time many of these mountains are volcanic, and about once every five years there is a major eruption in Iceland. The islanders still recall the eruption of Laki in 1783, which produced the greatest flow of lava ever recorded by man and caused a bluish haze in the sky that was seen all over Europe, and even as far as western Asia, and lasted throughout the summer. In Iceland this haze stunted the grass crop, causing a famine which resulted in the death of 9,000 of the islanders and three-quarters of their sheep and horses.

Fortunately, not all the eruptions are so harmful, and some may even be creative rather than destructive. One eruption in the sea off the coast of Iceland created an entirely new island. The hot springs and natural steam fields, which are also features of volcanic areas, are now being put to good use by the islanders. In Reykjavik this hot water is piped and used for domestic supply and to fill the town's swimming baths.

Iceland is a young country compared with most European countries (The first people came to settle there only about 1,000 years ago during a period which is called the 'Settlement Time' (AD 870–930). Many of these settlers were Vikings from Norway, who came to Iceland at the same time as other Vikings were attacking the eastern shores of

Britain. At that time there was not only no human habitation on the island, but also very few animals and those of only one kind – the arctic fox. There were birds in abundance, however, especially ducks and geese, which still breed in Iceland today.

Iceland may also be said to be young in another sense. While in Europe many of the valleys that once contained glaciers have now lost much of the characteristic shape of a glacial valley through the action of rainwater and wind, in Iceland the passing of the glaciers from the valleys that are now inhabited took place only comparatively recently. In consequence the countryside has a rough-hewn appearance, the deep valleys still retain the U-shape of the typical glacial valley, and in many places the land remains as bare of earth and plant life as it was when the ice of the glaciers was grinding slowly over it.

Today there are still large areas of semi-desert, even in the lowlands, and there are very few trees. It is said that at the 'Settlement Time' the land between the coast and the mountains was thickly wooded, but that this wood was soon used up and destroyed by the settlers. The Icelanders are now wisely beginning to replant the land with trees.

Where the glacial valleys reach the coast they were flooded by the sea, and the mountains that formed the valley sides drop sheer into the water. These sea inlets, known as fjords, are also a feature of the coast of Norway and of the south-west coast of South Island, New Zealand. Most of the Icelanders live on isolated farms or in scattered villages either on the valley floors near the heads of the fjords, or on the spits of shingle which thrust out from the sides of the fjords, built up by the action of the sea currents. Most of these farms are on sites that have been occupied since the 'Settlement Time', surrounded by a patch of cultivated grassland, the farmer sharing with his neighbours the rougher land towards the interior for summer

Vestmannaeyjar, a busy fishing port on one of the islands off the southern coast of Iceland. The fish-processing plants are grouped around the inner harbour so that the catches can be processed as soon as they are landed from the trawlers

Hot springs are a feature of some parts of Iceland and are put to practical use in heating water for domestic supply

grazing. The manured land near the farm provides grass for winter feeding.

Grain is difficult to grow, so the farmers depend very largely on their livestock. This consists mainly of sheep – there are twelve times as many sheep as there are cattle and dairy cows. Horses are grazed on the northern uplands even though they are rarely used today for transport purposes or farm work; many people ride them for pleasure and they are invaluable in the autumn when the sheep have to be rounded up from the wild uplands of the interior. The farmers too have found a way of putting the hot springs to good use. The water is piped into greenhouses and keeps them so warm that even tomatoes and cucumbers can be grown.

The seas around Iceland are very rich in fish, for it is in these coastal waters that the cod, haddock, saithe and whiting come to spawn. The catching and processing of fish employs about 14 per cent of the islanders, and fish are a vital part both of their own food and of their exports. The great diesel trawlers that have replaced the open boats of a hundred years ago catch, in the main, cod, herring, saithe, capelin and redfish. When the fish reach land they go to the processing plants, where as little as possible is wasted – there are factories for making fish-meal, refineries for codliver oil, and much of the fish is filleted by machine and quick-frozen for export. So important is the fishing industry to Iceland that she has felt she must take steps to protect her interests. Though she has been a member of the European Free Trade Association since 1970 agreements with the European Economic Community have been held up until the settlement of the dispute on fishing rights.

Many other industries also centre round the fishermen – the shipyards and engineering works where the trawlers are built, and the factories that make fishing gear. Many of the other industries on the island are new, for example, the manufacture of cement, a commodity which, until recently, was imported. This is a vital material in a country where there is little timber for housebuilding, and no building stone or clay for bricks. An example of an old, established industry is printing, for the islanders are voracious readers, and Iceland produces more books per person than almost any other country.

Until the end of the nineteenth century there were only two ways to travel in Iceland – by packhorse over the mountains and along the coast, or by one of the coastal vessels that sailed from port to port. It was not until 1880 that the first wagon road was built. During the present century there has been a tremendous effort to bring roads to all the small hamlets of Iceland, though there will probably never be a road along the south coast where it would soon be destroyed by the glaciers and the powerful streams. Hundreds of bridges have had to be built, but now, though the roads are narrow and only surfaced with gravel and volcanic slag, there is at least a communications system. In addition there is an internal airways system, taking in many of the outlying places as well as providing regular flights between such industrial centres as Akureyri and Reykjavik.

NORWAY
Kingdom
Area: 324,000 sq. km/125,000 sq. miles
Population: 4,000,000   Capital: Oslo
Flag: Red with blue cross bordered white

Norway is very long but very narrow and is nowhere wider than 435 km (270 miles). Her frontier runs from the entrance of the Baltic Sea along the ridge of mountains that divide her from Sweden, across the top of Finland through Lappland, and is finally shared with the USSR until it reaches the Barents Sea, far north of the Arctic Circle. To the west lies the Norwegian Sea and a coastline of islands, large and small, of mountains falling steeply to the sea, and of deep fjords cutting into the central mountains. Thanks to a branch of the North Atlantic Drift, the coastal areas of Norway have a fairly mild climate, though inland, where the warm currents have less effect, the weather is much harsher and there are many glaciers in the higher mountain areas.

Norway has been a settled country for a long time. Bronze Age rock carvings of ships have been found that may date as far back as 1500 BC. It was

from here that the Vikings set out in the ninth century in search of riches in other lands, for the population had grown too large to support itself in a country that had, and still has, very little agricultural land. Even today, only 3 per cent of the total land mass of Norway is under cultivation, though there are other extensive parts of the country where trees can be grown. So it is not surprising to find that the settlement pattern in Norway is much the same as in Iceland. The villages and towns are found near the heads of the fjords, on the islands, on the narrow strips of hummocky lowland known as 'strand flat' along the western seaboard or in one of the three small lowland areas – around Oslo and Trondheim or near Stavanger.

The great length of the country and the variety of the terrain give rise to great regional variety in climate. The North Cape, 'the Land of the Midnight Sun', has long arctic winters in which the sun never appears to rise from mid-November to late January, while, in summer, the sun remains above the horizon from May until July. The weather changes rapidly over short distances and from season to season everywhere in Norway, and while the heat may become trapped between the rock walls at the head of a fjord, in a sunless hanging valley nearby the snow will remain all the year.

Agriculture provides a living for about one-fifth of the Norwegian population, but their produce is not nearly sufficient to feed the whole nation. Fish, milk, and meat are abundant, but the low temperature makes it generally impossible to grow grain, though there are exceptions to this in the three productive areas mentioned above. In the Oslo district (Ostlandet), the farmers grow potatoes, and a state subsidy helps them to produce barley, oats and wheat, but cows and domestic animals are a greater source of income. In Jaeren there are early potatoes and vegetables, and tomatoes and cucumbers are grown under glass. The oven effect of the mountain walls in the southern fjords often makes it possible to grow apples, pears and plums.

Outside these fertile areas, the general pattern is of very small mountain farmsteads (saeters) where the farmers used to make their own butter and cheese, but now send their milk to the dairies in the valleys if they are lucky enough to be connected by road. Often these farms do not provide a sufficient living for their owners, who accordingly take up

ICELAND

Reykjavik

0   200   400   600 *miles*
0   400   800   1000 *kilometres*

FAEROE IS.

LOFOTEN IS.

NORWEGIAN

SEA

Kiolen Mountains

Trondheim F
Trondheim

N
O
R
W
A
Y

Jostedals Bre

Galdhöpiggen
8097

Sogne F

Bergen

Hardanger F

Oslo

S
W
E
D
E
N

Stockholm

L. Vänern

Göteborg

GOTLAND

ÖLAND

FI

A T L A N T I C   O C E A N

SCOTLAND

Edinburgh

5

Belfast

REPUBLIC
OF
IRELAND

Dublin

UNITED

Manchester

N O R T H

SEA

DENMARK

Copenhagen

BALTIC SEA

LIT

Gdansk

WALES

Birmingham

KINGDOM

ENGLAND

London

Amsterdam

Southampton

Hamburg

Elbe

Berlin

P O L A N D

GERMANY

WEST

EAST

Leipzig

Oder

Warsaw

Wroclaw

Vistula

4

Brussels

3

Bonn

Rhine

Frankfurt

*Moravian
Heights*

*Bohemian
Forest*

Prague

CZECHOSLOVAKIA

Cracow

BAY OF

BISCAY

Paris

Seine

6

Black Forest

Danube

8

Munich

Vienna

Nantes

F R A N C E

Loire

Vosges

Zürich

Bern

Innsbruck

AUSTRIA

HUNGARY

Budapest

Jura

Geneva

7

Lyons

Drava

Zagreb

Danube

Bordeaux

Lascaux

*Massif
Central*

Rhône

Mt Blanc
15782

Alps

Milan

Turin

Venice

Po

Sava

YUGOSLAVIA

Belgrade

Cape
Finisterre

Cantabrian Mountains

AltaMira

Bilbao

Toulouse

Cévennes

Pyrenees

2

9

Nice

Genoa

Florence

Apennines

Rome

Dinaric Alps

ADRIATIC SEA

Dubrovnik

Oporto

Duero

Ebro

Maladeta
11168

Zaragoza

P
O
R
T
U
G
A
L

S   P   A   I   N

Madrid

Tagus

Barcelona

Marseilles

I
T
A
L
Y

Tiber

*Tyrrhenian
Sea*

Tirane

10

Pinc

Lisbon

Guadiana

Valencia

CORSICA

Naples

Pompei

Sierra Morena

Guadalquivir

Cape
St Vincent

Sevilla

Mulhacén
11420

Murcia

*BALEARIC
ISLANDS*

SARDINIA

Cádiz

Málaga

Sierra Nevada

1

M E D I T E R R A N E A N

Palermo

Etna
10741

SICILY

*Ionian
Sea*

MALTA

SEA

N O R T H   A F R I C A

BARENTS SEA

Kanin Peninsular

Kola Peninsula

WHITE SEA

• Archangel

URAL MOUNTAINS

Sverdlovsk

Europe

L.Onega

EUROPEAN PLAIN

UNION OF

SOVIET SOCIALIST

| 1 GIBRALTAR |
| 2 ANDORRA |
| 3 BELGIUM |
| 4 NETHERLANDS |
| 5 NORTHERN IRELAND |
| 6 LUXEMBOURG |
| 7 SWITZERLAND |
| 8 LIECHTENSTEIN |
| 9 MONACO |
| 10 ALBANIA |

L.Ladoga

Gulf of Finland

Leningrad

Kazan

Volga

ONIA

Kuybyshev

• Moscow

Volga Heights

REPUBLICS

•••• = THE BOUNDARY BETWEEN EUROPE AND ASIA

Smolensk •

Central Russian Uplands

Ural

A

• Vilnius

Dnieper

• Minsk

ARAL SEA

BYELORUSSIA

Pripet

Pripet Marshes

Desna

Volga

Astrakhan •

Kiev •

UKRAINE

Don

• Rostov

MOLDAVIA

Odessa •

Dnieper

Sea of Azov

CASPIAN SEA

MANIA

Crimea

Caucasus Mountains

Elbrus ▲ 18480

• Bucharest

Danube

BLACK SEA

GEORGIA

• Tbilisi

AZERBAIJAN

Baku •

• Sofiya

Yerevan •

ARMENIA

BULGARIA

Ararat ▲ 12945

• Tabriz

ECE

Istanbul •

Bosporus

L.Van

• Tehran

Salonika •

Ankara •

Kizil Irmak

Sakaria

T U R K E Y

L.Tuz

Erciyas ▲ 12850

AEGEAN SEA

Athens •

Toros Mts

Tigris

• Aleppo

Baghdad •

RHODES

Euphrates

I R A N

CRETE

• Nicosia

CYPRUS

SYRIA

I R A Q

Basra •

The Sogne Fjord in Norway. The west coast has deep fjords cutting into the mountains which run down the whole length of the country

part-time occupations. In the North the cold, dark winters make work on the land impossible, and the farmers join in the cod fishing off the Lofoten Islands, while in the south many of them are foresters as well as farmers, owning their own small plantation or helping in the state-owned forests.

Even forestry is a partly seasonal occupation, though the seasons for this are largely traditional. When the logs had to be dragged by horses, the foresters preferred to do this in winter when the snow on the ground and the frozen bogs and lakes made it easier for the horses to move them. Today most of the cartage is done by trucks and lorries, and the many new roads have reduced the extent to which logs have to be dragged across rough country. The logs felled are then floated down one of the main rivers, or towed across one of the larger lakes, for processing.

The Norwegians have for long been great fishermen, and, since the Second World War, have doubled their annual catch. Herring make up the greater part of this catch. Until recently herring catching was a very risky business, for it was never possible to predict when and where the shoals

would arrive, and a spell of bad luck over a period of years could bring ruin to a fishing village. Today there are research vessels which locate the shoals in the late autumn and follow them with Asdics and echo sounders until they are within reach of the fishermen.

Herring are generally caught by purse seiners or drifters. The purse seine, a net 365m (200 fathoms) long, is set out in a ring around a herring shoal, drawn together at the bottom, and hauled up on the mother vessel – the purse seiner. She is helped in this operation by a smaller auxiliary vessel. The drifter, on the other hand, works with more than a hundred drift nets of 27m to 33m (15–18 fathoms) length, which are linked together and kept floating at the right depth by buoys and lines. The purse seiners take the greater part of the catch, though they cannot be used in high seas and are useless when the shoals are very deep. The drifter, a smaller boat, is still useful under these conditions.

Cod is the other important catch. It used to be centred almost entirely in the Lofoten Islands, but Finnmark is now becoming rather more important. The boats and crews are small compared with the herring fisheries. Most of the fishermen also have small farms in Nordland (the mainland area on the arctic circle) and merely stay in Lofoten for the cod season, when some of the villages have ten times their normal population.

Norway is not a land rich in minerals, but there are important iron ore and pyrite mines and copper concentrates are also produced. Limestone is quarried, mainly in Ostlandet, and used in the manufacture of nitrogen fertilizers and cement, and in Vestlandet and Nord-Norge there is quartz to be found.

Undoubtedly the greatest natural resource of Norway is water. The high rainfall in the mountains and the deep, steep-sided valleys are the essential conditions for the production of hydro-electric power – the valleys are more easily dammed than broader valleys would be, and the supply of water is assured, though the snow may make it rather seasonal. Ninety-nine per cent of Norwegians have mains electricity – a remarkable achievement in a country where there are so many remote farms and villages – and the cheap and plentiful supply of electricity has encouraged the development of large industries, especially electro-chemical and electro-metallurgical industries. The latter produce, for example, aluminium and steel. The bulk of the raw materials has to be imported, and so the factories are generally found on the fjords where both power and transport are close to hand. The electro-chemical industry is generally based on domestic raw materials that are close to hand, and produces, among other things, carbide, cyanide, nitrates and artificial fertilizers.

Water power was used as long ago as the six-teenth century to drive saws in sawmills, and today the wood processing plants that produce wood pulp and paper are still to be found by the great water-falls, for it takes up to 100 tonnes of water to pro-duce one tonne of wood pulp. Fish processing is also an important industry, though the old tradi-tional methods are still often used: klippfish, for example, is salted and left on the bare rocks to be dried by the sun and the wind, and herring are salted in barrels. But some klippfish is now artifici-ally dried, the herring may be used to make herring meal or herring oil, and the cod are increasingly being fast-frozen for export. The enormous fleet of Norwegian merchant ships helps to compensate for

the fact that Norway has to import so much more than she can export. She earns foreign currency, not by carrying goods to and from Norwegian ports, but by carrying them between other foreign countries. The oil-tankers play a very important part in this, plying between the Persian Gulf and the Caribbean oil-ports. Norway is a member of EFTA (see entry on Denmark) but rejected membership of the EEC in a referendum held in 1973. A special relations Trade Agreement was, however, signed with the EEC in the same year.

Communications have long been a problem in Norway, for not only is it difficult to build railways and roads across high mountains and deep valleys, but much of the area between east and west Norway, especially in the north, lies under deep snow from November to May. Formerly, the sea was the most important thoroughfare, for it was always open, and it still provides the only passage

A steelworks on the Arctic circle. The plant uses hydro-electric power as Norway has no natural coal deposits

The screen-like construction on the left of the picture is the traditional method of drying cod in Norway and is still widely used despite the growth of modern techniques

Lapp tents in Altafjord, Norway

in some areas, notably between the mainland and the islands and between the shores of the fjords. Regular boats still serve the ports along the coast, travelling Norway's 'Royal Road'. Where the calmness of the water can be counted on, fast hydrofoils are used. But roads and railways have also been built, the railways with considerable difficulty and expense. Consequently the railway network is small though very impressive. One branch line runs from the Bergen-Oslo railway on the high plateau down to Flam at the head of Sogne Fjord, a distance of only a few kilometres, in which it falls 900m (3,000 ft), cutting backwards and forwards through the rock face of the glaciated valley. This must certainly be one of the most impressive pieces of railway engineering in Europe.

SWEDEN
Kingdom
Area: 450,000 sq. km/174,000 sq. miles
Population: 8,100,000   Capital: Stockholm
Flag: Light blue with yellow cross
To the east of Norway, and occupying the larger part of the Scandinavian peninsula, is Sweden, a country which is in a much more favourable economic position than her neighbour. There are far more extensive supplies of minerals, and most of the deposits are far richer, especially those of iron ore. Sweden's forests of fir and birch cover about half the surface area of the country, and are the main reason why Sweden has become a much richer country than Norway, with a standard of living as high as any other country in Europe.

A typical mountain landscape in the north of Sweden

Though there are mountains and glaciers in the north, the landscape in the south is generally low lying and the rainfall much smaller, as the winds of the North Sea are nearly dry after crossing the Scandinavian Highlands. Grain crops, root crops, potatoes and grasses can all be grown, though most of the farmers rely on dairy produce for their living.

Farmers began to settle here and to raise crops and livestock about 3,000 BC. In the first century AD the Roman historian Tacitus mentioned a tribe called the 'svear' who lived in eastern Sweden. They founded many of the village settlements that still exist today. These people were great seafarers, like the other Scandinavian peoples, and in the ninth and tenth centuries, when southern Sweden belonged to Denmark, they took part in the Viking raids on Britain and Western Europe. Sweden was still, at the time, inhabited by a number of distinct tribes, though they all had the same king and met once a year at Old Uppsala to make sacrifices to their gods.

It was not until the end of the Viking raids that Christianity got a firm footing in Sweden, but in 1164 the first Archbishop was established at Uppsala and churches, at first of wood but later of stone, began to be built. The Swedes conquered Finland and in the 1250's the new city of Stockholm, in a central position between the two, became the capital of the kingdom. By the middle ages Sweden had already become an important trading centre, and copper and iron was being mined in the hills.

A wood pulp mill at Soraker Sweden. After felling, the trees are floated in great raft down the river from the fore to the mill

Piled logs waiting for the ice to thaw before starting their journey down the river

In the seventeenth century, Sweden became one of the strongest powers in Europe, pushing her borders eastwards. She was allied to France in the Thirty-Years War, and added to her territory large areas of northern Germany by the Treaty of Westphalia. Changes were taking place at home too. Mining methods were modernized and an important weapons industry grew up. The Swedish aristocracy built magnificent mansions and castles for themselves, many of which can still be seen, and the talented Queen Christina even made Sweden an artistic centre before her abdication in 1654.

The new era began at the end of the eighteenth century. Sweden had by now lost her status as a world power and begun to pay more attention to her internal problems. When the French marshal, Jean Bernadotte, became King of Sweden in 1818 he decided that in their foreign policy the Swedes should remain neutral, and this has been an established policy ever since. Sweden began to co-operate with her Scandinavian neighbours in every kind of activity, while at home the government of the country was reformed and the landowners, merchants and factory owners wielded power in place of the aristocracy. Toward the end of the

century agriculture was modernized and Sweden fast became an industrialized and urban country. In 1972 a special Trade Agreement was reached with the EEC.

FINLAND
Republic
Area: 360,000 sq. km/139,000 sq. miles
Population: 4,700,000   Capital: Helsinki
Flag: White with blue cross, the upright to the left of centre

Finland, unlike Norway and Sweden, is predominantly a low-lying country. Not only is this landscape more suitable for agriculture because it is flat but also because, following the last ice-age, the lowland area was flooded by the Baltic Sea which, when it retreated, left behind it a fertile sediment. Yet only a small percentage of the land is used for grazing and crop growing, for Finland is a place of forests and lakes. Coniferous forests cover about 70 per cent of the land, and many of the Finns are involving in the felling of these trees and in floating them down the rivers or towing them across the lakes to the mills where they are cut into planks or pulped. Wood and its products – pulp, paper and

A typical landscape in northern Finland. Countryside like this inspired the music of Jean Sibelius, Finland's great national composer

cardboard – are Finland's most significant exports, though the metal and engineering industries and dairy and other agricultural products are also important. The domestic requirements of the Finns – for foodstuffs, textiles, plastics, etc. – are generally met by their own domestic production.

Finland is in many ways an isolated country. The sea along her southern and eastern coasts freezes solid in the winter, though the main ports are usually kept open by icebreakers. To the north lies the wasteland which is inhabited only by the Nomadic Lapps, and to the east the long frontier with Russia. But Finland's isolation is decreasing, as her trade expands both with eastern and western countries. Helsinki, the capital, is only 310 km (190 miles) by sea from the great Russian city of Leningrad, which buys Finnish butter, iron and iron products, and ships such as ice-breakers and trawlers.

DENMARK
Kingdom
Area: 43,100 sq. km/16,600 sq. miles
Population: 5,000,000   Capital: Copenhagen
Flag: Red with white cross left of centre
Denmark, the last country we have to consider in Scandinavia, is made up of a peninsula and a group of islands large and small at the entrance to the Baltic Sea. The country is flat and its greatest natural resource is not mining or forestry, of which there is little, but the quality of the land. Nearly half of the land area of Denmark is used for cereal crops and root crops and a further quarter for green fodder and grasslands. We have been talking of countries where much of the land is of no use at all, except as an attraction for tourists, land permanently covered by snow, land too steep for soil to lie on it and land where the vegetation is too thin to support animals. In Denmark there are some infertile areas of heathland and sand dune along the western seaboard, and a few areas of marshland, but this only accounts for 7 per cent of the countryside and the remainder is all exploited. What is not used by the farmers is forested or is occupied by buildings, gardens or roads.

Many of the farms in Denmark are part of larger co-operative concerns. A group of farmers club together, share in the expense of buying machinery and stock and also share the profits in proportion to the amount they have contributed. This process began in Denmark in the nineteenth century when co-operative dairies and co-operative bacon factories were set up. The system has made farming much more profitable than it would have been if the farmers – most of whom have smallholdings of between 10 and 60 hectares (25 and 150 acres) – had continued to work independently. Today, there are co-operative cow-houses, co-operative feedstuff companies and common pools of machinery.

Denmark also is affected by the North Atlantic Drift which assures her warmer winters than one would otherwise expect in a country as far north as this. Though there are usually about a hundred nights of frost per year, rye and wheat sown in the autumn usually survive the winter and are ready for harvesting during the following August and September. But most of the corn is sown in the spring and harvested in the late summer. One of the factors that makes the weather rather unreliable in Denmark is that it is here that the warm westerly winds from the Atlantic often meet the polar winds that blow from the east, and this causes rapid changes in temperature. Nor is the rainfall ideal for growing crops. Little falls in May and June when the corn needs watering while heavy rainfall in the autumn makes harvesting difficult.

Most of the crops grown in Denmark are used as animal fodder. The most important animals kept by the farmers are cattle and pigs, and their products are a very important Danish export.

While the greater part of Denmark continues to be under cultivation, the labour force needed in the farms has decreased thanks to the introduction of machinery and the amalgamation of many of the farms into co-operatives. About 40 per cent of Danes are now employed in industry and trade, though in many cases this means that they are engaged in processing the farmer's produce – conserving meat, fruit and vegetables, refining the sugar beet, or using the barley crop to make Tuborg or Carlsberg lager. Denmark has certain other useful raw materials to hand, apart from the forests which cover only a small part of the land surface in comparison with the other Scandinavian countries. Boulder clays – deposit left by the retreating ice-cap at the end of the ice-age – are used to make bricks and tiles; white chalk is an ingredient in the manufacture of cement; and the

A view over the roof-tops of
Copenhagen, the capital of
Denmark

Rich agricultural land in Jutland, Denmark

island of Bornholm provides both clay, for the potters' use, and granite, for building stone houses and surfacing roads. Otherwise, Danish industry depends heavily on foreign supplies, both for the raw materials with which the factories work, like iron and chemical raw materials, and for machinery and the fuel on which it is run. If Denmark had continued to rely on the export of agricultural produce she would not have been able to afford expensive purchases of foreign raw materials; but today many of these materials are re-exported in the form of manufactured goods, earning for Denmark the foreign currency she needs.

Together with Great Britain and Ireland, Denmark became a member of the European Economic Community (EEC) in 1973. The Danish people confirmed their country's membership in a referendum. Denmark is also a member, together with Iceland, Finland, Norway and Sweden, of the Nordic Council, which agrees on free trade between the countries and has abolished work permits.

UNITED KINGDOM
Kingdom in Commonwealth
Area: 244,700 sq. km/94,500 sq. miles
Population: 55,900,000   Capital: London
Flag: Union Jack

The United Kingdom consists of the countries of England, Scotland and Wales, together with the northern part of Ireland (Northern Ireland or Ulster). Each country sends representatives to the central Westminster government. However, Scotland and Wales have become dissatisfied with the government in London and there are plans for devolution, that is the establishment of separate elected assemblies in Edinburgh and Cardiff which would be given considerable control over the internal affairs of each country. Northern Ireland had its own parliament at Stormont, but this was suspended in 1972 because of widespread internal sectarian troubles.

SCOTLAND
Country in UK
Area: 78,700 sq. km/30,400 sq. miles
Population: 5,200,000   Capital: Edinburgh
Flag: White diagonal cross on blue ground St Andrew's cross)

Geographers ordinarily divide Scotland into three zones – the Southern Uplands, the Lowlands and the Highlands and Islands. These are satisfactory as very general divisions, though a closer examination of each area will soon reveal far greater variety. The Highlands, for example, are taken to include all the land that lies north of the Highland Line, the foothills that stretch along the northern sides of the Clyde and Tay valleys. This is an area of hill, mountain, moor and loch, often picturesque for the tourist but in the main a difficult land for the farmer, who relies mainly on raising sheep for his income.

The Highlands are cut into two by the Great Glen, a long, steep-sided valley that runs from Inverness on the Moray Firth to Fort William at the head of Loch Linnhe. For much of its length the glen is filled by long narrow lochs, one of which, Loch Ness, is 39 km (24 miles) long, little more than 1·5 km (1 mile) wide, and goes down in places for 240m (800ft). The wind, driving down the funnel-like glen, often gives rise to strange patterns of foam on the surface of the Loch, and this may be the key to the stories of the Loch Ness Monster. The Monster, whether he is real or imaginary, attracts many visitors to this beautiful wooded spot. One of the few important working canals in the country runs down the Great Glen, joining the east coast to the west coast, saving ships the long journey round the Pentland Firth and through the islands on the west coast.

The highlands of Scotland form one of the two extensive mountainous areas in Great Britain. The other being in Wales. To the east of the Great Glen lie the Grampian Highlands, an area of rounded hills and moorland, with villages and farms clustered in the sheltered land on the floors of the glens. Occasionally, the mountains rise to impressive heights. The Cairngorm Mountains, which reach their highest point in Ben Macdui 1,309m (4,296 ft), provide some good climbing country and are becoming a popular area for skiing, especially since the building of a large, modern skiing centre at Aviemore. To the west lies Ben Nevis, the highest mountain in Britain 1,343m (4,406 ft). The mountains of Glen Coe are much steeper and craggier and hang darkly over the glen which is a favourite place for rock-climbers. Whisky is produced in the northern part of the Grampians, and the drink

Edinburgh Castle, seen from Princes Street

continues to be a very important export, especially to the United States. Many of the ports have fishing fleets whose main catch is the herring.

The country to the west of the Great Glen is rougher, and here it is even more difficult to make a living from the land, except in the few favoured lowland areas. As a result, both here and in the islands, the population has been steadily decreasing in the rural communities, for there is no work for the young people. New industries have been introduced to the area, like the atomic-power plant at Dounreay and the distillery at Invergordon;

whisky is one of Scotland's most important exports, large quantities going to Japan. However a great deal more needs to be done if this part of the Highlands is not merely to become the home of the deer, the grouse and the occasional shepherd with his flock. Many of the Hebridean Islands specialize in the way they earn their living. On Harris and Lewis, in the Outer Hebrides, it is the production of tweed – generally called 'Harris' tweed, though it is produced in both parts of the island. It is well-known for its warmth and hard wearing quality. Fishing boats put out from Stornoway, and sheep

The shores of Loch Lomond at Luss,
Dumbartonshire, Scotland

are kept on the hills as elsewhere in Scotland, but much of the land cannot be made productive because it is covered in a thick layer of peat. The islanders dig the peat up in small slabs like a turf. When dried it burns slowly and warmly on a fire. The people of Islay, in the Inner Hebrides, make whisky, while Skye is the most popular of the islands with tourists.

The Shetland Islands form the most northerly county in Scotland; there are over 100 islands and islets, covering some 1,400 sq. km (550 sq. miles). The chief town is Lerwick. About one-third of the land is cultivated; although the climate is damp and mild, agriculture is limited by strong winds. The Shetlands are famous for ponies and sheep; the wool has given rise to a flourishing cottage industry producing woven and knitted woollens. The population, however, is declining.

The Orkneys, over 70 islands separated from mainland Scotland by the Pentland Firth, are intensively cultivated, exporting large quantities of eggs and growing barley for distilling.

One of the most important recent events in Great Britain has been the discovery and development of large oilfields in the North Sea, off the coast of Scotland and north-east England. The first oil was brought ashore in 1975 and it is hoped that eventually sufficient oil will be pumped ashore to be of real assistance to the economy and to enable Britain to cut down on oil imports.

The southern Uplands are made up of a number of small groups of hills. In East Lothian and Berwickshire there are the Lammermuir Hills, south of Edinburgh the Pentland Hills, the Lowther Hills in Lanarkshire, the Rhinns of Kells in Kirkcudbrightshire, and the Cheviot Hills running along the border with England. Conditions are much better for farmers here, and there is some excellent farming country both in the glens and in the lowland areas along the coast. The main east-flowing river is the Tweed, a world-famous salmon river. Thanks to the excellent pasture for sheep on the hills and the availability of water in the tributaries of the Tweed, this area is the home of important woollen industries, with Hawick at the centre of the trade. In many ways this area has more in common with the counties of England than with the Highlands, in appearance and in the way of life. It was colonized by the Celts who occupied Wales and by the Anglo-Saxons who conquered England in the sixth century. The Highlanders, on the other hand, are descended from the Picts, the oldest inhabitants of Scotland, the Celts who arrived in the Bronze Age, and the Scots, a Celtic tribe who came from the north of Ireland.

The narrow strip of lowland Scotland that runs from Glasgow to Edinburgh and the Firth of Tay is the industrial and economic heart of Scotland. Glasgow, on the Clyde, has a population of over a million, and its port and the satellite towns on the estuary of the Clyde are together one of the chief commercial and trading areas in the world. Apart from its port, Glasgow is well-known for ship-building and it is possible to launch very large ships into the Clyde estuary.

Edinburgh, the capital city, is much smaller than Glasgow (less than half a million) but is the business centre of the Kingdom and a university town. A large area of the centre of the city was replanned towards the end of the eighteenth century and rebuilt in the Georgian style and much of this has been preserved. Some original sixteenth century buildings remain in the old part of the city near the castle. Below the castle, at the foot of the 'Royal

Mile', as it is called, is the Palace of Holyrood, where Mary Queen of Scots resided for a time. Scotland is also an important centre of the arts, having a permanent opera company based in Glasgow, and a national ballet. Edinburgh is the home of the internationally famous Festival of the Arts, held each summer.

ENGLAND
Country in UK
Area: 130,400 sq. km/50,300 sq. miles
Population: 46,400,000   Capital: London
Flag: Red cross on white ground (St George's cross)

The Thames has for long been the most important of England's rivers, and London lies on the upper tidal reaches of the river. It was already a busy trading city early in the first century AD, and was the centre of Roman power in Britain. The capture of London from the Danes by King Alfred dealt a very heavy blow to the Danish chances of conquering the whole of Britain. London grew in power and was very jealous of its independence. The form of administration of the present square mile known as the City of London owes much both to Saxon and to early Norman precedents. The Common Council, composed of the Lord Mayor, the Aldermen and the Common Councilmen, is derived from the Saxon *folkmote*; and the annual election of the Mayor dates from 1215, when King John granted a charter authorizing the practice, though the title 'Lord Mayor' was not used until the fifteenth century. The office of Alderman is also Saxon in origin. Aldermen were at first elected annually, but Richard II commanded that they should be chosen for life.

London today, of course, has expanded far beyond the original bounds of the city walls. London was still quite a small place, by modern-day standards, at the beginning of the nineteenth century. While the old city remained the commercial centre, residential buildings had spread westwards and builders such as John Nash in the eighteenth century had built fine terraces of houses, separated by broad streets quite different from the narrow overhanging alleyways of the old city. As the nineteenth century passed, London expanded in all directions, and places that had once been only villages on the outskirts suddenly found themselves

This street, consisting of terraced houses and a modern block of flats, is typical of many areas of London

part of one great city. This process of expansion is still continuing today. Since the Local Government Act of 1963, the overall ruling body for the whole London area has been the Greater London Council, which has taken the place of the old London County Council and Middlesex County Council. The Greater London Area has a population of nearly eight million and covers 1,580 km (610 sq. miles).

London, besides being the capital and centre of government of the United Kingdom, is also headquarters of the Commonwealth Secretariat. The Commonwealth is an association of 34 independent member states, eighteen of them republics, and sixteen monarchies (eleven of which recognize Queen Elizabeth II as Head of State).

Many people believe that London has been allowed to become too great. They are thinking not only of its physical size, but of the fact that it overshadows other parts of the country in business and as a cultural centre. Its size, of course, does create considerable problems, not least that of transport. Partly because of the high price of living accommodation in the centre of London, but also because of the noise and dirt, most Londoners live in the outer suburbs while working in central London; the

A typical shopping street in one of the older London suburbs

A view looking over Trafalgar Square with the National Gallery lower left and the church of St Martin-in-the-Fields centre left

Part of the rugged coast of north Cornwall

movement of this enormous body of people into London in the morning and out at night overtaxes both the rail and the road transport systems, making living conditions on the main traffic-carrying routes even more intolerable for residents and movement along the roads very slow. Though the construction of new underground railway lines (the Victoria line was completed in 1971 and the first stage of the Fleet line is nearing completion) will relieve some of this crush, the real remedy is to encourage offices to move outside London. Many have already done so, helped by government grants. Industry, too, is moving out of London and much of the centre and east of the city is now very sparsely populated. With the closing of the great docks plans are being drawn up for rebuilding and new uses for the areas.

The higher wages of the capital attract people from all over the country, especially from the poorer areas where employers cannot afford to compete with London wages. As a result, London and the south-east, already the richest area of the country, become richer as they attract the talented people and the money that is needed to make industry expand; while the poorer areas only get poorer and suffer depopulation and decline. This applies to the arts too. London possesses the finest museums, the finest collections of paintings and sculpture, most of the important theatres and two opera houses. It is hardly surprising that those who live outside London, whose taxes help to support all these institutions, should become angry when they find that they are too far away to make any regular use of them.

If London dominates the country as a whole, there still remain some important local centres which have a strong pull in their own areas. York is still the capital of the North, or so they would say in the north-east, anyway. York was the base of the Roman Ninth Legion (who called the town Eboracum), and in AD 306 Constantine was proclaimed Emperor here. In the seventh century, York was the capital of a kingdom – known as Northumbria – which dominated the rest of England at a time when the country was divided up into a number of small Saxon kingdoms. Northumbrian monks illuminated the Lindisfarne Gospels, one of the most beautiful medieval books: it can still be seen today in the British Museum. Conquered by the Danes and badly damaged by the Normans, York had once again become a thriving market town by the fourteenth century, and one of the chief cities of the medieval wool-trade. It continues to flourish today, producing chocolate, scientific instruments, sugar and glass containers, and making rolling stock for the railways.

York is a fine city to visit, for though the modern industries thrive here many signs survive of the interesting past she has enjoyed. Most impressive of all, perhaps, is the Minster, the largest cathedral built in England in the middle ages, covering an area of 5,662 sq. m (60,952 sq. ft). Begun in the early thirteenth century, the Minster was not finished until the mid-fifteenth century; so it covers three periods of medieval architecture. Many of the windows contain finely designed and coloured medieval glass, made by local craftsmen. The massive medieval walls of the old city with

Harvesting wheat with a combine harvester. Agriculture in England is highly mechanized

their gates or 'bars' are still standing, and, within, there are Tudor, Stuart and Georgian houses, a castle on a mound built by Henry III and known as Clifford's Tower, a fine museum, an art gallery, and many churches.

The city of Bristol lies 10 km (6 miles) from the mouth of the Avon and the Bristol Channel. It was a royal borough even before the Norman Conquest and in 1373 Edward III, in a charter, granted it county status. Its position on the Avon made it an important seaport, and in the eighteenth century it became the chief port in the trade with the West Indies. This was the centre of the sugar trade and the tobacco trade, and cigarettes are still manufactured here from imported tobacco. Bristol was very badly damaged during the Second World War, but some of the fine buildings from her past still remain. The Avon runs through a deep gorge on the seaward side of Bristol which is spanned by a suspension bridge completed to the designs of I. K. Brunel in 1864. It is 214m (702 ft) long, and was, in its time, regarded as an engineering miracle. Modern freight ships, of course, need a greater depth of water than the ships of the eighteenth century, and the Avon is not deep enough to carry

the larger ships to Bristol any more. Most of them now dock at Avonmouth or Portishead and the closure of Bristol Docks is planned to take place in the late 1970's. Today's main imports are cereals, tea, cocoa and coffee, molasses and sugar, fruit and frozen meat, metals, ores and chemicals, tobacco, wines and spirits.

Manchester was still a village while Bristol was becoming a great seaport. The Cathedral was originally the Parish Church. But the Industrial Revolution transformed both Manchester and the neighbouring towns and villages, as the development of the cotton industry turned farm workers into factory workers and villages into huge areas of sprawling terraced houses. Manchester was eventually named a city in 1853. Today it is primarily a commercial centre, not a manufacturing town. The work of production is far more the concern of the many towns in the vicinity of Manchester. There are to be found the engineering works, the chemical plants and the textile factories, while Manchester handles the packaging and distribution of goods

Camping in the beautiful Langdale Valley in the Lake District of England

A typical English rural landscape

and deals with banking and insurance. The Manchester ship canal was opened at the end of the nineteenth century to link the city with the sea. Manchester has become a thriving and lively city, and, as well as being a commercial centre, is also the entertainment and cultural centre for the area. There is the city's own orchestra – the Halle – the excellent art gallery, the university, and the many artistic and scientific societies. The *Guardian*, though a national newspaper today, originated as the daily newspaper of the Manchester area.

National Parks include the Lake District whose highest point is Scafell Pike 964m (3,162 ft), and this is a fine area for walkers and climbers, but the mountains are confined within a comparatively small area. There are many other areas of hill and fell however, the most distinctive being the Pennine Chain, which runs from the upper reaches of the Tyne to the Peak District of Derbyshire. The fast streams that flow down from the Pennines to the Irish Sea provided the motive power for the cotton industry that developed in Lancashire in the nineteenth century to become one of the most important manufactures in the country and a key factor in the transformation of England from a primarily agricultural to a primarily industrial country. East of the Pennines lie the North Yorkshire Moors. The two other upland areas are in the West country – Dart-

moor and Exmoor. Other ridges of high ground strike off at an angle to the general direction of the Thames Valley – the Cotswolds and Chiltern Hills towards the north-east, and the North Downs, Forest Ridges and South Downs towards the south-east – while Salisbury Plain dominates the country that separates the Thames Valley from the valley of the Bristol Avon.

WALES
Principality in UK
Area: 20,760 sq. km/8,000 sq. miles
Population: 2,800,000   Capital: Cardiff
Flag: Red dragon on white and green ground
Though Wales has been one kingdom with England since Edward I conquered the country at the beginning of the fourteenth century, the Welsh have nevertheless retained their separate identity, and the partnership with the English has not always been to their mutual satisfaction. During the late middle ages disaffected Welshmen often joined in rebellions against the English crown when the opportunity arose and nationalism is intense in Wales as in Scotland. The Welsh language, which has never died out in many parts of the country, particularly the north, is undergoing a revival and all schoolchildren are taught to speak it. National bardic festivals are becoming increasingly popular

A concentration of heavy industries, coal-mining and steel-making, in South Wales

and many more people are studying Welsh literature and writing in Welsh.

Most of Wales is mountainous. Snowdon reaches a height of 1,085m (3,560 ft) and Cader Idris 892m (2,927 ft). Further south there is the range dominated by Plynlimon 752m (2,468 ft), and the Black Mountains and the Brecon Beacons. The Severn, the longest of the English rivers, begins in Wales on the slopes of Plynlimon and flows inland into Shropshire before turning south towards Worcester, Gloucester and the Bristol Channel. The Wye, famous for its salmon and one of the most beautiful of British rivers, also has its source in Plynlimon. It flows southwards between Radnor Forest and the Black Mountains and meanders down through Monmouthshire to the Severn

North Wales is famous for the beauty of its lakes and mountains

Estuary. Cardiff, the capital of Wales, has a population of a quarter of a million and sends four members to Parliament. Here there are large iron and steel works, rolling mills and foundries, as well as other industries such as breweries, jam factories, paint works and electrical goods. The nearby seaport of Swansea is the chief centre in Britain of the copper, tinplate and zinc industries, and coal, ores and oil pass through the port. Wales is by far the smallest of the three mainland countries of the British Isles, but is larger than Northern Ireland.

NORTHERN IRELAND
Region in UK
Area: 14,150 sq. km/5,460 sq. miles
Population: 1,500,000   Capital: Belfast
Flag: Red cross on white ground with emblem in centre

Northern Ireland, although part of the United Kingdom, had a separate Parliament and executive government, but in 1972, because of continued violence between sectarian factions, the British Government prorogued the Northern Ireland Government and introduced direct rule from London. The capital is Belfast, which has a population reaching nearly 400,000 and is an important seaport as well as possessing a large university and cathedral. Its chief industries are shipbuilding, aircraft manufacture, machinery, textiles and ropes. North of Belfast, near Portrush, lies the famous Giant's Causeway, consisting of enormous columns of basalt.

The greater part of Ireland is occupied by a central limestone plain, with occasional hill and mountain groups, primarily around the coast. The highest of these ranges is Magillicuddy's Reeks – Carrantuohill is, at 1,041m (3,414 ft), the highest point in Ireland. The principal river in Ireland is the Shannon. It flows 385 km (240 miles) through a series of loughs to Limerick, and from there to the West Coast. Partly because of the moderating influence of the Atlantic, the climate of Ireland is less extreme than that of Great Britain.

IRISH REPUBLIC
Republic
Area: 70,300 sq. km/27,100 sq. miles
Population: 3,000,000   Capital: Dublin
Flag: Green, white and orange vertical bands

The early history of Ireland is shrouded in legend, but at about 500 BC the country was divided into eight kingdoms, the rulers of which acknowledged the authority of the 'High King' of Tara. There followed a long period of internal strife, punctuated by the Norse invasions. Nevertheless, the land of saints and scholars helped to keep learning alive in the British Isles. In 1155 Ireland was ceded to Henry II by the Pope, and so began the bitter anti-English feeling which lasted until the present century, culminating in the Easter Rebellion of 1916. The Home Rule Act was passed in 1920 and in 1921 the Republic of Eire achieved independence.

The capital city of Eire is Dublin. It has grown up around the castle, and contains a great deal of magnificent eighteenth century architecture. There has always been much rivalry between its two seats of learning, Trinity College and University College, though the latter is in the process of moving to a site outside the city. Dublin is also the centre of a number of light industries as well as having a large brewery. It is the largest town in Ireland with a population of 567,866.

Like Dublin, the city of Cork in the South grew rapidly in the seventeenth and eighteenth centuries, though it suffered heavily in the Great Famine of 1847. Today it has a large export trade, mainly of agricultural products, as well as other industries. A few miles from Cork lies Blarney Castle, which houses the famous Blarney Stone.

Perhaps the most famous of Ireland's tourist areas is Killarney, site of the celebrated Lakes. These lie in the County of Kerry to the south-west of the country. Another area of interest is the Arran Islands, off the West Coast, where a primitive fishing economy is still practised in bleak conditions. On the mainland lies the historic town of Galway, sited on both sides of the River Corrib which is renowned for its salmon fishing. To the North of Galway lies the district of Connemara.

NETHERLANDS
Kingdom
Area: 33,800 sq. km/13,100 sq. miles
Population: 13,400,000   Capital: Hague (Amsterdam)
Flag: three horizontal bands of red, white and blue

Examination of a map of the Netherlands shows

Polderland, a typical Dutch landscape. The windmills house pumping stations to keep the land drained

that one-fifth of the country lies below sea level. The combination of stormy weather and a high tide could bring the water high enough to flood half the country. No other country has had a problem of this magnitude to deal with. How have the Dutch managed not only to keep back the floodwaters but also to claim land back from the sea and convert it into fertile crop-producing soil?

As far back as the thirteenth century, the Dutch began to build barriers against the sea, drain land and so create land from water. These new tracts of land they called 'polders'. At first these polders only consisted of quite small areas, but in the seventeenth century means were discovered of draining larger tracts of land: the invention of the rotating turret made it possible to point the sails of a windmill in any direction, according to the direction of the wind, and this constant power could be used to pump water out of flooded areas like lakes and marshes. In the mid-nineteenth century steam-driven pumps were first used to drain Lake Haarlem, south of Amsterdam. This not only assured the protection of the city and the surrounding country against flooding when there were gales, it also made available 19,000 hectares (47,000 acres) of new and fertile land. There is now an airport here, its control tower 4·5m (15 ft) below sea level. Land continued to be reclaimed throughout the nineteenth century, but the greatest advances have come within the last sixty years, and the two most ambitious schemes are still in process

of completion – the Delta Project, and the Zuyder Zee Works.

At the beginning of this century the Zuyder Zee was a deep inlet of the North Sea, its maximum width 59 km (37 miles) and its greatest length 80 km (50 miles). All round its edge, the land had to be protected by dams which, in bad weather, had to take the full force of the storms and tides. The first step in the project was to build a dam across the 32-km (20-mile) wide mouth of this inlet, a job which it took from 1927 to 1932 to complete. The Zuyder Zee, shut off from the open sea but fed by the inland rivers, gradually became a freshwater lake (now known as Lake Ijssel) capable of providing the surrounding provinces with water supplies in time of drought.

The approximately 290 km (180 miles) of inland dykes around the Zuyder Zee, no longer exposed to the ebb and flow of the North Sea tides, have been less expensive to keep up since the Barrier Dam was completed, and the dam also carries a district road link between the provinces of North Holland and Friesland. The level of water in Lake Ijssel is kept at about the same level as the mean sea level (half way between high and low water). At low tide the surplus water in the lake is drained off into the sea through sluices.

The next stage was to build the polders inside the freshwater lake. Now that the lake was no longer tidal, the task of building the new dykes was much easier. The first polder to be completed was

The port of Rotterdam, the greatest and busiest port in Europe. It serves all the countries through which the Rhine flows

the Wieringermeer Polder, an area of about 20,000 hectares (50,000 acres). First the dykes were built all round the area to be drained. Dredgers removed the soft mud from the sea bed where the dyke was to run, and filled this trench with sand, to give the dyke a better foundation. Parallel mounds of boulder clay were then built up along the outside edge of the foundation, forming the outer and inner sides of the dyke, while the trench in the centre was filled with sand to form the core. The part of the dyke that was to be submerged was protected by brushwood mattresses, covered with rubble, while the exposed slope was faced with stone where it was thought necessary.

The next stage was to set the two pumping stations to work. These took $6\frac{1}{2}$ months to drain the area. Of course, the ground, even when it was drained, was still salty and infertile. The salt had to be washed completely out of the soil before the land could be used, and this was done by building a network of drainage trenches and drainage pipes throughout the area, and by lowering the water level in the ground to as much as 1.5m (5 ft) below the lowest point in the ground surface of the polder. Finally houses and farms were built and electricity and water supplies connected.

The first setback came during the war. The Germans, who were occupying Holland, discovered that the Allies were attempting an invasion and decided to flood the Wieringermeer by breaching the dykes on the lake Ijssel side. The inhabitants of the polder managed to escape, for it took two days for the area to flood completely, but nearly all the houses and farms were destroyed and lay under 4m (13 ft) of water. Work began on the breaches as soon as the Germans had capitulated, and, with the use of auxiliary pumps, the polder was drained within four months.

Two other polders are now in use. The North-East Polder is twice the size of the Wieringermeer and was drained in 1942. About 30,000 people now live and work here. Eastern Flevoland some 54,000 hectares (133,000 acres) was drained in 1957 and 85 per cent of the area is now under cultivation. Southern Flevoland 42,500 hectares (105,000 acres) became dry in 1968, and Markerwaard 60,000 hectares (148,000 acres) will be finished in 1978. Lake Ijssel will then cover about one-third of its original area, and narrow arms of the lake will continue to divide the last three polders from the mainland. This is because the ground water-level of these polders is so low (in the case of Eastern

Flevoland, between 5m and 6m (16–20 ft) below sea level) that if they were connected to the mainland it would cause the ground water-level there to sink considerably, and the crops would not be properly watered.

Thanks to the Zuyder Zee Project, the arable area of the Netherlands will have been increased by about 10 per cent, there will be new space for towns to relieve the congested areas of the country, new sites for industry, and new places for sailing, swimming and sunbathing for the holiday-makers.

BELGIUM
Kingdom
Area: 30,500 sq. km/11,800 sq. miles
Population: 9,800,000 Capital: Brussels
Flag: Three vertical bands, black, yellow and red

Belgium is one of the most densely populated countries in Europe. The most abundant raw material is coal and Belgium is also a major manu-facturer of steel. Like Britain, Belgium's industry is largely dependent on manufacturing goods from imported raw materials, and one of the most important of these is textiles, of which the best-known are woollens, lace and carpets.

Quite a large part of the working population is engaged in some form of agriculture and forestry; the latter in the Forest of Ardennes. Because of the flat, low-lying geography of large areas of Belgium many crops can be grown successfully, including grass for feeding beef cattle. Market gardening is also widely practised, especially around the out-skirts of Brussels.

The capital, Brussels, is in the province of Brabant and lies on the river Senne. The old or 'Lower' town has many outstanding buildings of historical interest and is still the centre of Belgium's commercial life. The 'Upper' town is the modern residential area but within it are many outstanding buildings, especially the Palais de la Nation, the seat of Belgium's parliament. Like most capitals Brussels has many thriving industries, especially

Antwerp, Belgium's largest seaport. It lies on the east bank of the river Scheldt. On the left of the picture is the 14th century Gothic cathedral

Harvesting flax on the banks of the river Lys at Courtrai, Belgium. The flax is processed in the linen factory in the background

A corner of Bruges, the capital city of West Flanders, Belgium. It is a medieval city with a fine cathedral and Gothic town hall

Pasture slopes in the Bavarian Alps

textiles. The famous battlefield of Waterloo where Wellington defeated Napoleon is only about nine miles from Brussels.

Two main languages are spoken in Belgium – Flemish (a form of Dutch) which is used by the Flemings who live in the north and French, used by the Walloons of the south.

Belgium was one of the earliest countries to enter into a special trade agreement with her neighbours, the Netherlands and Luxembourg (Benelux). Now the country is the seat of the headquarters of the European Economic Community and the Council of Ministers, both of which are based in Brussels. Luxembourg, a small Grand-Duchy situated be-

tween France, Germany and Belgium, is the seat of the European Parliament and the European Court of Justice.

GERMANY, FEDERAL REPUBLIC
Republic
Area: 248,600 sq. km/96,000 sq. miles
Population: 62,000,000   Capital: Bonn
Flag: Horizontal bands of black, red and gold
When we speak of England or Scotland, there is no mistaking where we mean, even if we are talking about the middle ages or the seventeenth century. Both countries are delineated mainly by their sea coasts, and what boundary there is between them

is short and has shifted little over the years. When we speak of Germany things are quite different. It is more difficult to form a mental picture of Germany for it is not a geographical entity. The sea is its boundary on only one side, the north. On the other sides it shares an artificial boundary with nine other countries and these boundaries have changed many times in the last thousand years or so.

Germany really started to exist as a unit in the year 800. During the two centuries before that date the Teutonic tribes in the area – Lower Saxons, Frisians, Franks, Thuringians, Alamanni and Bavarians – had been moving closer to each other, mainly because of two factors; in the first place,

their conversion to Christianity which was initiated by Irish monks in the seventh century; and secondly, the similarity between their languages. The year 800 is a convenient date to choose because it was then that Charlemagne was crowned Emperor at Rome, Emperor of an Empire that covered an area roughly the same as present day France, Germany and Italy, and the smaller countries that divide them.

Charlemagne's Empire was short lived, partly because he was not succeeded by anyone of the same calibre, but also because the Empire was really too big. It was impossible to administer such an area in the early middle ages because communica-

The Rhine near the Lorelei Rock, Germany. The terraced slopes on the far bank are vineyards

tions were too slow. The Empire was broken up, the eastern part passing at last to one Henry the Fowler, the first of the House of Saxony that was to rule Germany from 919 to 1024. During this period the tribes were united into one nation, but the Kings also began to get involved in affairs outside Germany. Otto III had himself crowned Emperor at Rome as Charlemagne had done, and later on, the Hohenstaufen Emperors spent more and more time in Italy, fighting wars with the Pope and his allies. Germany itself was bled of men and money for these wars, and the real government of the country passed into the hands of the counts, who gained almost complete control within their own areas. The dynasty of the Hohenstaufens ended with Frederick II (1194–1250), who hardly passed any time at all in Germany, preferring his residence in Sicily. Germany continued to expand, however, during the next two hundred years, and the lands beyond the River Elbe were added to the realm.

Germans continued to refer to their Kings as Emperors even after the passing of Frederick II. From 1438 to 1740 the German Imperial Crown was held by the Habsburgs. This was a period when many great artists and thinkers came to light – Erasmus, Albrecht Dürer, Martin Luther, Hans Holbein the Younger, Johann Sebastian Bach and Georg Friedrich Händel – but still Germany continued to shift her borders. At the end of the Thirty Years War (1618–1648) Switzerland and the Netherlands ceased to form part of the German Empire.

The Holy Roman Empire of the German Nation came to an end in 1806, a victim of the military strength of the Emperor Napoleon. Thereafter the German states formed a loose association, known at first as the German Federation. This came to an end in 1866 when Austria, which had been the leading power among the German states for five hundred years, seceded. The new association was

A typical agricultural village in the Rhineland

The Rhine Plain near Dortmund, where rich agricultural land surrounds busy industrial towns

The busy shipyards at
Hamburg on the north bank
of the Elbe

Duisberg on the river Rhine

A view of the old part of
Hamburg

called the North German Federation and in 1871 it became one empire with the King of Prussia as Emperor.

At the end of the Second World War, the territory of the former Nazi Reich within the 1937 frontiers was divided up into four zones of occupation by the Allies (Britain, France, Russia, the United States). The former capital, Berlin, was to be governed jointly by these four powers. The eastern provinces of the Reich came under Polish rule. In 1949 the French, British and American Zones of occupation became the Federal Republic of Germany, an independent and democratically ruled state, whose seat of government is at Bonn. This country is generally referred to as West Germany, while East Germany is another name for the German Democratic Republic, a communist-ruled state, closely associated with the USSR, which administers the former Russian Occupied Zone. Berlin, which lies within the Eastern territory, remains the nominal capital of both countries. It is divided into East and West Berlin by a concrete and barbed wire wall erected by the Eastern authorities in 1961. Allied troops remained in West Berlin after the end of the war so as to preserve its independence.

Although German industry suffered extensive damage during the Second World War, particularly in the area of the Ruhr, rebuilding and reconstruction began shortly after the war ended and Germany has now become the most important industrial country in Europe, with a stable economy and a high standard of living.

FRANCE
Republic
Area: 544,000 sq. km/213,000 sq. miles
Population: 52,300,000   Capital: Paris
Flag: Blue, white and red vertical stripes (the tricolour)

In France there is as much variety of landscape as there is in the whole of the rest of Europe. There are the many mountain areas: the jagged peaks of the Pyrenees that stretch along the border between France and Spain; the French Alps, in which lies Mont Blanc 4,810m (15,781 ft) and the glaciers that run down from it, and countless winter skiing resorts; and the Massif Central, a large area of hummocky limestone mountains west and south of

Lyons through which hard volcanic rocks have been forced to form isolated peaks and craters. The sea coast in the north of France is much like the south-east coast of England – chalk cliffs and pebble or sand beaches – but as one progresses first westward and then southward it gradually changes: in Brittany there are small sandy bays and rocky promontories, the rocks sometimes of a deep glowing red colour; on the Atlantic coast, long straight sandy beaches backed by pine forests; and along the Mediterranean the dazzling light and the bright colour contrasts that gave rise to the name Côte d'Azur – the Azure Coast – and attracted first artists and later yachts, casinos and playboys.

There is as much change and contrast inland; between, for example, the rocky hills of Provence and the Rhône valley where the grapes are grown for the famous wines of Provence and Burgundy, and the plains of the Beauce, south-west of Paris, stretching as far as the eye can see, bearing in summer a heavy crop of grain. Everywhere there are signs of the long and varied history of this part of the world. Near the south of the Rhône, aqueducts, theatres, and arenas still survive from Roman times; at Lascaux, prehistoric paintings have been discovered in a cave, and in Brittany a structure known as a 'dolmen' – two upright stones supporting a large flat stone – is evidence of a civilization similar to that which erected the prehistoric circle at Stonehenge; there are also the châteaux or castles of the Loire, many of which were possessed by the English kings in the twelfth century when

The Donzère-Mondragon hydro-electric power station in the Rhône Valley

The nuclear power station at Chinon in the Loire Valley

most of northern and western France was in English hands. Everywhere there are old churches, many of them as much as 700 years old.

France was in a very poor state by the end of the Second World War. Her industry was in ruins, many of the towns and cities in the north had been largely destroyed by bombing, and the country was bankrupt. The problems of reconstruction were enormous. Ninety-five per cent of the great port of Le Havre was in ruins, and neither the port of Bordeaux nor that in Marseilles had a single crane in working order. These problems were eventually overcome. The towns and ports were rebuilt and

industry returned to normal. But France has managed to do more than just this. She has also transformed herself very rapidly into a modern country, founding new industries and modernizing her agriculture. Many people see this rapid recovery as nothing short of a miracle.

As in Britain, many new ways of producing power have been developed. During the 1950's coal was the main source of power, and the French coalfields were exploited as fully as possible to fulfil the demand. Now that alternative sources of power have been found, coal production is being run down. Natural gas has been found at Lacq, at the foot of

Rough cattle pastures in the
Massif Central

A view of Les Baux, north-
east of Arles

A water pumping station in Languedoc. This is part of a large project to use the waters of the Lower Rhône, especially for irrigation

the Pyrenees, and at Saint-Narcet; the total amount of natural gas produced in 1973 was over 7,500 million cubic metres. Nuclear power stations have already been built, and there are more to follow. The rivers are used to produce hydro-electric power, and not only the rivers in the mountain areas of the Massif Central and the Alps. Some 130 km (80 miles) from its mouth, the Rhône has been used for one of the largest schemes in France undertaken by the Compagnie Nationale du Rhône. The River Rhône has always been an important highway, especially between Arles, near its mouth, and Lyons, the chief city of southern France. But it was very risky navigating the stretch between the towns of Donzère and Mondragon where the river meandered over a flat plain, for it divided into small subsidiary streams and was obstructed by islands and banks of shingle. This whole area has now been transformed. Some of the waters of the river have been redirected into a specially built canal, about 29 km (18 miles) long, deep enough for the ships bound for Lyons to pass through it. There is only one lock on this canal, where it has to by-pass the barrage that has been built to convert the flow of water in the canal into hydro-electric power. This flow is kept even, as is the depth of water in the

canal, by controlling the amount of water that is allowed to flow into the old bed of the river. Much of this water is used for irrigating farm land in the area. Nearby, an atomic-energy centre has been built as part of this industrial complex.

Another interesting method of generating power is being tried on the Rance estuary near St Malo in Brittany. This sea estuary runs for some miles inland, and the high tides mean that a large body of water moves in and out of the estuary each time the water rises and falls. By building a barrage near the mouth the energy of this flow of water may be converted into electric power. This power station was the first of its kind to be completed in the world.

French agriculture provides further examples of the ability of the French to adapt themselves to new situations after working in much the same way for hundreds of years. Naturally, in a country stretching from the English Channel to the Mediterranean, there are great differences in temperature and rainfall as well as the differences in landscape that have already been mentioned. This gives rise to regional specialization – for example, olive trees and citrus fruits are grown particularly in the south, grain in the plains of the centre and north. These are the

The Renault car factory at Boulogne-Billancourt, on the river Seine

The region of Lorraine is rich in iron-ore, which is mined there

Mont Blanc on the frontier of France and Italy. The glacier
is the Mer de Glace, formed from two glaciers, the Giant
Glacier on the right and the Leschaux Glacier on the left

The Île de la Cité, Paris. On the centre right of the island is the cathedral of Notre Dame

areas where these crops can be grown best, though corn, for example, can be and is grown in almost every part of France. In most parts of the country one hectare (2½ acres) of land will yield about 2·5 tonnes of wheat, while in the plains north of the Loire and in Flanders and Picardy one hectare will produce as much as 4 tonnes.

An entirely new crop in France is rice, first introduced here just after the Second World War. In the flat plains of the Rhône delta, where large supplies of water are at hand, rice grows excellently and enough is now produced to supply the whole of the needs of France.

Fruit and vegetables are eaten a great deal in France, and the public demand a high standard. This has also led to specialization, with intensive farming of a particular crop by scientific methods. There is, for example, specialized market gardening along the coast of Brittany. There may be specialization in both fruit and vegetables within the same area, as in the Nord region, the Paris region, the east, the Val de Loire, the Rhône valley near Lyon,

the Mediterranean coast, the Garonne valley and the Roussillon.

Everywhere in France, livestock, particularly cattle, are becoming more important to the farmer than growing vegetables are. France is the chief cattle producing country of the Common Market. There are beef herds in the Limousin and Charolais areas and dairy cattle in the Hollandais area, while dual breeds are also becoming popular. One of the side products of the dairy herds is the many varieties of cheese that come from the provinces – among them Camembert, Brie and Roquefort.

It was the French Foreign Minister, M. Robert Schuman who, in 1950, initiated the pooling of the French and German coal and steel industries, which later led to the formation of the European Economic Community in 1957, with six member countries – France, Germany, Belgium, Italy, Luxembourg and the Netherlands. In 1975 three more countries, Britain, Denmark and Ireland also became members. The aim of the EEC, or Common Market, is to unite these countries – together with

A typical scene on the Channel coast of France

others which may eventually join them – in a common policy covering industry, agriculture and in time the monetary system. Two other bodies, the European Coal and Steel Commission (ECSC) and Euratom, which deals with international atomic matters, are now included in the EEC. Trade agreements have been made between the EEC and many non-member countries in Europe. In 1963 at Yaoundé (Cameroun) an agreement was signed between 18 ex-colonial African states and the EEC, covering overall trading and economic co-operation. A further treaty, covering 42 developing countries was signed at Lomé (Nigeria) in 1975. Details of the countries affected are given under CAMEROUN and NIGERIA. Negotiations are taking place with Latin-American countries with an aim to agreements in the future.

SWITZERLAND
Confederation
Area: 41,300 sq. km/15,900 sq. miles
Population: 6,400,000   Capital: Berne
Flag: Red ground with white cross
Switzerland is a predominantly mountainous country in the centre of Europe. It is completely surrounded by land frontiers with France, Germany, Austria and Italy. It has a long tradition of

political freedom and has had the status of a republic ever since it was formed in 1847. Seventy-three per cent of the country is covered by land classed as mountain and although mountain pastures are used extensively for the raising of cattle there remains only a very small land area available for agriculture. Large parts are also forested – almost a quarter of the total land area. As a result the industries of Switzerland are those which occupy only a small amount of space and demand special skills, such as electrical engineering and watchmaking. However the major occupations are banking and insurance, for which Switzerland is a world centre. Tourism also makes further use of the physical resources of Switzerland. The beauty of the Alps has attracted visitors for many years and mountaineers have always come to Switzerland to climb the Alps and the Jura mountains. More recently the increasing interest and enthusiasm for skiing has brought thousands more visitors to Switzerland to ski on the lower Alpine slopes throughout the winter when the resorts of most countries are empty.

Switzerland is divided into 'Cantons' or states, which together make up the confederation. These have often strongly individual characteristics and their dividing lines often match language differences. There are three official languages, French,

Cattle grazing high up in the
Swiss Alps

A field of wheat near Lake
Geneva, Switzerland

German and Italian and parts of Switzerland contain populations speaking each language. There is also a fourth national, but not official, language, Romansch, but this is only spoken in very few places. German is the dominating language in nineteen of the cantons, French in five cantons, Italian in one and Romansch in one.

ITALY
Republic
Area: 301,000 sq. km/116,000 sq. miles
Population: 54,900,000   Capital: Rome
Flag: Green, white and red vertical stripes
The shape of Italy is very familiar to most people. If you look on a map you will see that it is like a high-heeled boot stretching out into the Mediterranean Sea from the south coast of Europe. It is a peninsula jutting out from the mainland and cut off from the surrounding countries by the Alps. The area administered by Italy also covers as many as seventy islands in the Mediterranean, some of them large, like Sicily and Sardinia, and many others, which are uninhabited, too small to show on most maps. A map which shows land heights reveals very clearly which are the principal regions of Italy. You

can see the mass of the Alps which protects Italy from the harsh climate of Northern Europe and shelters the northern plain. South of the Alpine border with France, Switzerland and Austria is the flat fertile plain of the river Po in Lombardy. Here is some of the richest agricultural land in Italy, as well as some of Italy's loveliest cities. Venice, Padua, Mantua and Milan all owe their origin to the fertile land that surrounds them and in the west lies Ravenna, the capital of the Byzantine Empire in Europe with its buildings decorated with some of the loveliest mosaics in the world.

South of the Po delta the great chain of the Apennines stretches down the length of Italy, where land over 300m (1,000 ft) above sea level covers the majority of the country. Here, in Central Italy, are the greatest towns of the nation, Florence, Rome, Perugia, all containing some of the most beautiful buildings and paintings in the world, centres of learning in the Middle Ages and slowly recovering some of their earlier fame today. The soil in most of the Apennines is poor, except for that around the Arno and the other river deltas of the west coast. The south of Italy is the poorest area. There the soil is thin and there are few raw

Lucerne, on the lake of the
Four Forest Cantons

A glacier in the Swiss Alps

In Tuscany land is still
cultivated by ox-drawn
ploughs. The chief crops are
grapes, wheat, maize and
potatoes

Newly developed farms near
Paestum, southern Italy

The popular holiday resort of
Salerno, southern Italy

113

materials; the people are very poor and live by fishing and farming. The region suffers from continual depopulation as the younger people leave for the thriving cities of the north.

Rome, the capital of Italy, is also the largest city with a population of almost three million people. The next largest towns are the great industrial centres of the north: Milan with a population of $1\frac{3}{4}$ million, Turin and Genoa of about one million, though Naples in the south has $1\frac{1}{4}$ million. Although more people are flooding into the towns Italy is still very much a country of scattered small towns and villages. The fact that until a hundred years ago the land covered by Italy was a number of small states is probably the reason why no larger centres of population have developed; also of importance is the fact that Italy's industrial development is very recent. The first industrial development in Italy took place in the period between the wars when Italy was governed by Mussolini in a form of Fascist dictatorship. The foundations were laid of the new roads and train services which are so essential in developing a primarily agricultural country and a beginning was made on industrial development. The Second World War prevented these plans coming to fruition and after the war the complete devastation of much of Italy's resources, both economic and agricultural, made vast redevelopment necessary. The development of agriculture in the north was followed by that of industry. Milan, Turin, and Genoa are all centres of industrial development, and attract vast quantities of workers to the new factories. Shipbuilding is one of Italy's expanding industries. The importance of shipbuilding emphasizes the importance of the sea in Italy's economy as a means of transport and a source of food. The chief mineral found in Italy is the natural gas deposit discovered after the war in the Lombardy plain. However, a certain amount of sulphur and lignite in the south and iron ores, lead, zinc and aluminium are also mined. Italy also produces a quarter of the world's supply of mercury. In Massa Carrara the famous coloured marble used extensively during the Renaissance is quarried. Out of a total labour force of twenty million, 20 per cent still work on the land, a further 45 per cent work in all kinds of industry. While the complex of development in the north around Milan, Genoa and Turin is still the centre of heavy industry a new plant is being established in the Puglia district in the south centred on the large nationalized steelworks at Taranto. Further development in the south is expected after the discovery of oil in Sicily. The need for power controls one of Italy's main imports, that of coal, but this is steadily being cut down as the products of the natural gas fields are being fully exploited and new hydro-electricity plants brought into use. The chief manufactures are concerned with engineering and the production of motor vehicles, textiles, iron and steel and steel products, building materials, and light machinery. There are also the kinds of consumer production familiar to any industrialized country in which high industrial wages provide a large market for goods. The

The city of Naples, one of the chief ports in Italy. In the background is the active volcano, Vesuvius

The scrubby landscape of the Gran Sasso Massif in southern central Italy

products of Italian light engineering are very famous; typewriters, domestic equipment and cars are among some of the largest exports. The Fiat car and the Olivetti typewriter are known all over Europe. Italian clothing, especially shoes and knitted garments, is well known for its design and quality. The worldwide inflation of the 1970's, however, affected the Italian economy very adversely.

Agriculture is still the main industry, although it employs only one-fifth of the labour force. Its main products are cereals, fruit, olives, cheese and wine. The dry sandy soil of the Apennines is especially suited to producing wine which is drunk in large quantities; large amounts are also exported. All over the countryside in Italy you can see the careful terracing of all available land to provide soil for growing vines. The olive trees also flourish in thin soil and there are few houses in the country which do not possess at least one olive tree to produce the oil which plays such an important part in the diet of most Italians. Dairy cattle are few and their products are expensive; although numbers are increasing, most of Italy lacks the rich grass necessary for the best cattle and large quantities of beef are imported. Fishing is carried on extensively from the small villages all round the coasts and from the large

ports, but the industry is declining and increasing quantities of fish are having to be imported. The most important crop is sugar beet which supplies most of Italy's needs and provides work in sugar refineries.

The contrast between the resources and the potential of the north and the south of Italy has been a source of concern to Italian governments for many years. The soil in southern Italy is too thin to be very productive and the region lacks the areas of fertility provided by the river deltas in the north. Shortage of water is a constant problem for farmers and one bad summer can be disastrous for farmers working on or near the poverty line. The south has no centres of industry and as the farming industry becomes more mechanized and the population expands there are fewer jobs than ever available to the younger people when they leave school. This acute shortage of work inevitably means that the young people move away from southern Italy in search of jobs in the prosperous north. The government is trying to counteract this tendency to drift north by encouraging the development of new factories and industries in the south to keep the young in their homes.

One of Italy's major industries that we have

St Peter's in Rome, with its cupola designed by
Michelangelo and its square by Bernini. The Obelisk came
from Heliopolis and once stood in Nero's Circus

ever is Italy's store of artistic treasures. The oldest
are the Etruscan tombs at Tarquinia outside Rome
where the visitor can see paintings on the walls of
underground tombs as clear as they were when first
painted in the centuries before Rome was great. In
the south there are many reminders of the days of
Greek and Roman civilization, of which the most
famous is the city of Pompeii, buried in AD 79 by
the eruption of Vesuvius. It has since been exca-
vated and is one of the most complete examples of
a Roman city anywhere in the world. In Rome itself
with the Colosseum and the Forum is preserved a
large part of the centre of ancient Rome as well as
the legacy of the Renaissance in such masterpieces
as the Sistine Chapel ceiling painted by Michelangelo and the collection in the Vatican Museum.
North from Rome are the many beautiful old towns
of Umbria, each with its great church or cathedral
and an ancient centre where the Italians still gather
to talk in the middle of the day as they have done
for centuries. Florence, probably the most beautiful
of all Italian towns, contains so much that many
visitors go only to Florence and spend their holiday
visiting all the many art galleries and museums
which the town contains, some of them, the Uffizi
and the Pitti, among the largest and most famous in
the world. Architecture is another constant interest
in Italy, and the visitor can see all kinds of building
from the early, simple shrines in small towns in the
hills to the great masterpieces of St. Peter's in
Rome, St. Marco in Venice and the Duomo in
Florence. All of them display some of the Italian
genius for building which makes nearly all Italian
towns pleasant and beautiful places.

Some of Italy's history is evident from the Italian
language. It is a romance language descended from
Latin. With very close links with classical Latin,
especially in its vocabulary, it is so similar that
anyone who is fairly good at classical Latin can
learn Italian with comparative ease. Italian literature has produced some of the finest writing in
Europe. The work of Dante in the fourteenth
century was followed by the writings of Machiavelli
on statecraft in the sixteenth century; these became
famous throughout Europe. The great Italian
universities at Padua, Perugia, Siena and Rome
have histories that stretch back through six
centuries and in the Middle Ages they were centres
of learning that drew scholars from all over Europe.

scarcely mentioned is based on the history of the
country. Over 35 million visitors a year pour into
Italy to look at the wonders of Ancient Rome,
Mediaeval Italy and the Renaissance. Catering for
this vast tourist trade, whether in the provision of
camping sites and youth hostels or luxury hotels,
provides a large number of Italians with very
profitable employment. Italy's historic interest is
not her only advantage – she also enjoys a warm,
mild climate, for she is sheltered by the Apennines
and the Alps, and has a long, sandy and rocky
coastline which provides almost unlimited bathing
facilities for visitors. The greatest attraction how-

The Bridge of Sighs in Venice, built between 1483 and 1498. Venice is built on a number of small islands in a lagoon and transport within the city is by boat, no cars being allowed. Every year Venice sinks a little further into the sea, but efforts are now being made to save the city before it is too late

The ruined Greek temple at Paestum, Italy

AUSTRIA
Republic
Area: 83,800 sq. km/32,400 sq. miles
Population: 7,500,000   Capital: Vienna
Flag: Red, white and red horizontal bands
Like Czechoslovakia, Austria formed part of the old Austro-Hungarian Empire and was established as an independent state after the First World War in 1918. At the end of the Second World War, Austria was divided into four occupied zones (Great Britain, America, France and Russia), and recovered her independence in 1955. Vienna, the capital, has always been a centure of culture, especially music – and in particular the music of Mozart, Beethoven, Schubert, Brahms and Mahler. If you look at the map you can see that it has boundaries with a large number of other countries; Czechoslovakia, Italy, Hungary, Germany and Switzerland. Although the population is small the country is very mountainous so that there is little flat land for settlement, and communications are difficult. Agriculture is the major occupation, producing crops and livestock, and there are vineyards too. Timber occupies 38 per cent of the land area of Austria and is a valuable source of wealth. There are also heavy industries centred around the iron ore deposits and the oil deposits found in Eastern Austria. Hydro-electric power is being developed in the mountains.

The countries of Eastern Europe became associated with and dependent on the Soviet Union after the Second World War. In recent years these ties have become less stringent; in fact, countries like Yugoslavia although Communist are wholly independent.

CZECHOSLOVAKIA
Republic
Area: 127,900 sq. km/49,400 sq. miles
Population: 14,600,000   Capital: Prague
Flag: Two white and red horizontal stripes, blue triangle next to staff
Czechoslovakia lies in the middle of Europe surrounded by Germany, Austria, Hungary and

Saint Anton in the Tyrol, Austria, is a ski resort

A large steelworks at Nova-Huta in Poland, the most industrialized country in Eastern Europe

Poland. The state which was established in 1918 was invaded by Hitler in 1938 and 1939 and occupied for the duration of the war. As a result the country suffered considerable hardship and at the end of the war was in a state of economic collapse. The post-war Communist government instituted a series of five-year plans to establish a Communist economy. During the 1960's the strict controls over action and speech began to weaken and in January 1968 pressures for reform resulted in the removal of the Secretary of the Communist Party, Novotny, and his replacement by the moderate Alexander Dubcek, who began to introduce new laws to ensure greater democracy and liberty of action. However, the Soviet Union, believing that this would affect other Communist countries, invaded Czechoslovakia with Soviet, Polish, East German, Hungarian and Bulgarian troops, forcing the Czech leaders to return to a hard line policy; and the new reforms were abandoned. Czechoslovakia now consists of the Czech Socialist Republic and the Slovak Socialist Republic, each of which has its own government, responsible to the legislative body, the National Council. Education is compulsory from the ages of six to fifteen, the basic five

year schools teach nearly two million children while there are a further $\frac{3}{4}$ million at secondary and technical schools, out of a total population of nearly fourteen million. The six universities in Czechoslovakia are free and open to all. The oldest of them is the Charles University in Prague which was founded in 1348; there are also many other institutions with university standing with nearly a hundred thousand students. Agriculture is one of the primary occupations in Czechoslovakia, and the many colleges train the farm workers in modern methods of production.

POLAND
Republic
Area: 313,000 sq. km/120,000 sq. miles
Population: 33,400,000   Capital: Warsaw
Flag: Horizontal stripes, white (above) and red

Polish recorded history begins only about the tenth century, when Christianity was introduced. In the twelfth century constant fighting occurred between Poland and Prussia. In the fourteenth century the Polish Queen, Jadwiga, married the Grand-Duke of Lithuania and so united the two countries. By the

A Polish peasant farm in the Beskids Mountains

growing such crops as wheat, barley, sugar-beet, potatoes and the like. Stock raising is also important. Since the war great strides have been made in improving industry, particularly heavy industry and the country has important mineral reserves, especially coal.

HUNGARY
Republic
Area: 93,000 sq. km/35,900 sq. miles
Population: 10,400,000   Capital: Budapest
Flag: Red, white and green horizontal stripes
Before the First World War, Hungary formed part of the Austro-Hungarian Empire. In 1920 it became a kingdom and after the Second World War, a republic dominated by the Soviet Union. In recent years Hungary has become more independent and self-sustaining. Like Czechoslovakia, Hungary attempted, in 1956, to break away from the hard-line policy of the Soviet Union, but the uprising was crushed by Soviet troops.

Like most Eastern European countries Hungary is mainly an agricultural country but making great efforts to improve its heavy industry. It has deposits of coal and bauxite, the ore from which aluminium is extracted.

The capital, Budapest, is one of the most beautiful cities in Europe. It sits on the Danube and is really two cities, Buda on the west bank and Pest on the east bank. It is the main trading centre of Hungary and such industries as chemicals, textiles and machine tools are carried on there.

ROMANIA
Republic
Area: 237,000 sq. km/91,700 sq. miles
Population: 20,800,000   Capital: Bucharest
Flag: Blue, yellow and red stripes with emblem in centre band
The name Romania comes from 'Roman' and in Roman times much of it formed Roman provinces. In modern times most of what is now Romania was ruled by Turkey until 1866. It became an independent kingdom in 1878. After the First World War the size of the country was greatly increased, Transylvania being taken from Hungary and given to Romania. After the Second World War the country ceased to be a kingdom and became a Communist republic. Bessarabia and North Buko-

sixteenth century Poland had become a powerful country. Russia began to interfere in Polish affairs and in 1772 Poland lost part of her territory to Russia, Austria and Prussia. By 1795 Poland had ceased to exist as a separate country, her territory being shared by these three countries. Poland gained her independence after the First World War, but in 1939 Germany attacked Poland and it was for this reason that Britain declared war on Germany.

Poland suffered immense devastation during the Second World War. The entire centre of the capital city, Warsaw, was wiped out and has since been very carefully reconstructed to replace the old town exactly as it was. The country relies heavily on its agricultural produce and has for some time been a major exporter of grain and dairy produce. The population declined by ten million during the war but has since increased and in 1973 was estimated at 33,500,000, 1/2 million less than the pre-war total. Similar reconstruction work to that in Warsaw has also been carried on in all other parts of the country. The many historic buildings which Poland possesses are being very carefully restored and the artistic heritage of the Poles is preserved and displayed in the magnificent state museums.

Poland is essentially an agricultural country,

vina, which had been part of Romania since the end of the First World War, were ceded to the Soviet Union.

Romania contains some of the richest grain-growing districts in the world and on the lower slopes of the Carpathians varied crops of fruits are grown. The country is also rich in such valuable minerals as gold, mica, natural gas and petroleum, especially the oil wells at Ploesti. Another important asset is the large area of forest which supports a thriving timber industry.

BULGARIA
Republic
Area: 110,900 sq. km/42,800 sq. miles
Population: 8,600,000   Capital: Sofia
Flag: White, green and red horizontal bands with emblem in top corner
From the fourteenth to the nineteenth century Bulgaria was dominated by Turkey, but in 1908 it became an independent kingdom. In 1946 the country became a republic within the Soviet sphere of influence. The nation is principally agricultural although in recent years it has been opened up to tourists with attractive resorts on the Black Sea. One of its best-known exports is attar of roses, an ingredient used by the perfumery industry.

YUGOSLAVIA
Republic
Area: 255,800 sq. km/98,800 sq. miles
Population: 21,000,000   Capital: Belgrade
Flag: Blue, white and red horizontal bands with five-pointed red star in centre
Yugoslavia was created in 1918 after the First World War. There had been two small countries – Serbia and Montenegro – and they joined together and, with some other territory that had formed part of the Austro-Hungarian Empire, formed the new state of Yugoslavia. It was a kingdom until after the Second World War when it adopted a Communist form of government under its war-time leader, Marshal Tito.

Yugoslavia is made up of six states: Serbia, Croatia, Slovenia, Montenegro, Macedonia and Bosnia-Herzegovina. The capital is Belgrade. Yugoslavia is a very mountainous country and it is one of those through which the River Danube flows. About half the people are farmers but the

A peasant farmer and his family going to market in Transylvania, Romania

The medieval walled town of Sveti Stefan, Yugoslavia, which has been developed as a tourist resort

country has many minerals, including coal, iron and lead. In recent years Yugoslavia has become a leading tourist centre with modern resorts along the whole length of its Adriatic coast.

GREECE
Republic
Area: 131,900 sq. km/50,900 sq. miles
Population: 9,000,000   Capital: Athens
Flag: Nine blue and white horizontal bands with white cross in corner on blue band

Most Greeks today are peasant farmers who grow and export tobacco and fruits; currants take their name from the city of Corinth where they were first grown. Much of Greece's income derives from the thousands of tourists who go to visit its magnificent antiquities, especially Athens the capital, whose people gave to the world the idea of democracy. There are also many islands, especially Rhodes and Crete, for the tourist to enjoy.

Because of the contribution of the Greeks to western civilization it may be useful to learn something of their history.

The Greeks of ancient times were divided into three great races – Ionians, Aeolians and Dorians. It was the Ionians of Asia Minor who first developed Greek science, literature and art. By 700 BC Greek trade was flourishing and the following century the city of Athens became the centre of Greek culture which was to influence European civilization for all time. The Persians, under Darius and Xerxes, tried unsuccessfully to conquer Greece. As a result of repeated attacks by the Persians the city states of Greece formed a confederation and this led to the building of an Athenian Empire under the Greek leader Pericles. But war developed between Athens and her rival Sparta. This war, the Peloponnesian War, lasted from 431 to 401 BC. The war was followed by the rise to power of Philip of Macedon and his son, Alexander the Great, who ruled not only Greece but a great empire that stretched into India. The Empire did not last long after Alexander's death and in 146 BC Greece came under Rome.

After the fall of Rome Greece was invaded by the Goths and Vandals, and in the sixth century by the Slavs. Greece formed part of the Byzantine Empire until the thirteenth century and in 1460 the country was conquered by the Turks. It remained under their rule until 1821. In that year the Greeks rose in rebellion against the Turks, but it was not till 1830 that Greece became completely independent. Greece became a monarchy after her liberation though some Greeks wanted a republic and this later on led to some trouble and discontent. In 1941 Italy invaded Greece and so Greece became one of the Allies. For a period after the war was over there was civil war in the country which added greatly to the sufferings of the people. Gradually Greece was able to recover and to rebuild the country. The king went into exile in 1967, and in 1973 the country was declared a republic. In 1975 a referendum was held on the restoration of the monarchy, but there was a large majority in favour of continuing as a republic.

SPAIN
Kingdom
Area: 505,000 sq. km/195,000 sq. miles
Population: 34,900,000   Capital: Madrid
Flag: Red, yellow and red horizontal bands with coat-of-arms on yellow band

Spain, a traditional monarchy, became a Republic under a Republican Socialist government after King Alfonso XIII left the country in 1931. In 1936 Civil war broke out, lasting for three years and culminating in the formation of a right-wing government under General Francisco Franco. In 1975, following the death of Franco, the country again became a monarchy under King Juan Carlos.

Though Spain is a European country occupying the greater part of the Iberian peninsula, her landscape has far more in common with the North African countries than with the countries of central and northern Europe. Much of the land is infertile and there is too little rainfall for the needs of farmers. If the cultivation of Spanish soil is to be made profitable, a great deal of hard work needs to be put into improving and irrigating it.

Spain's geographical separation from the rest of Europe – the chain of the Pyrenees mountains divides the Iberian peninsula and the south of France – has had its effect on her history and development. Industrialization has come only slowly to Spain and consequently her standard of living lags behind that of the other advanced western European countries. It is significant that Spain's greatest industry is her tourist industry, for

Rice fields in the flat, agricultural area of Valencia, Spain

The pattern of olive groves in Andalucia, Spain

not only has she the attractions of beautiful scenery, ancient towns, a peasant culture and sunny beaches, but also food, drink and accommodation are still comparatively cheap. The income from tourists in Spain forms an important item in the country's economy. Negotiations for association with the EEC were broken off in 1975 but resumed early in 1976.

The most fertile area of Spain is in the north, comprising the Basque Provinces, the Pyrenean region, Santander, Asturias and Galicia. The climate here is maritime, with mild winters, cool summers and heavy rainfall. The mountains are afforested, while in the valleys there are green meadows and orchards. South of this small area, across the Cantabrian Mountains, lies dry Iberia,

The port area of Bilbao (Spain) on the Nervión

These picturesque windmills are found on many of the Balearic Islands, especially Majorca and Ibiza

covering the rest of the country, including the high central plateau known as the Meseta. Here the rainfall is low and the summers hot and the rivers, especially those flowing east, are often quite dry for long periods in the year. Only when the rains come are the rocky, arid valleys suddenly filled with a rushing, and sometimes destructive, torrent. Olive groves are to be seen everywhere in the Mediterranean regions, as well as orange and lemon trees, fig trees and carob trees, and the small towns along the coast are centres for the fishermen who go out in their own small boats to catch lobster, crayfish, halibut and salmon. The Meseta is not unlike some areas of central Asia – an arid, rolling plain, comparatively featureless, bounded in the distance by rows of blue mountains. The long cold winters are a fierce contrast to the hot, dry summer months.

There are strong local traditions in Spain, many of which have survived into the twentieth century. Much of the traditional style of housing still survives. In the Pyrenean zone, the houses have sloping roofs to protect them against the heavy falls of snow. Country dwellings are usually built with two floors: a main floor or courtyard, where livestock is kept and where there is an oven for baking bread; and an upper floor, which is for the family alone and which comprises the bedrooms and perhaps a drawing-room. In Galicia and Asturias you may see a granary supported by four columns, known as a 'horreo', in which cereals, meat and game can be kept well-protected from damp and mice alike. Adobe houses, made of mud and straw, can still be seen on the Meseta. There is a curious heating system used in some Spanish houses: from a central hearth where straw is burned, ducts branch out under the tiles and distribute the heat all over the rooms. In La Mancha, Andalusia and the Levantine coastal regions it is customary to keep the outside walls of the houses cleanly whitewashed so as to provide protection against the heat of the sun. A patio, with a central fountain, is also a common sight in Andalusia.

Spain also has direct responsibility for the Balearic Islands and the Canary Islands, which are regarded as provinces. The Balearic archipelago is made up of the well-known holidaymakers' islands of Majorca, Minorca, Ibiza and Formentera, as well as a number of smaller islands. These islands have been colonized since prehistoric times and were occupied by the Romans after the fall of Carthage. The Canary Islands, an archipelago in the Atlantic Ocean off the southern part of the Moroccan coast, consist of seven inhabited islands and six islets which are uninhabited, divided into the two administrative areas of Las Palmas and Santa Cruz de Tenerife.

PORTUGAL
Republic
Area: 92,000 sq. km/35,500 sq. miles
Population: 8,600,000   Capital: Lisbon
Flag: Green and red vertical bands with national emblem

Portugal is on the west of the Iberian peninsula which she shares with Spain. The country is predominantly agricultural and over 40 per cent of the population is engaged in direct agriculture. It is a country in which extremes of poverty and wealth existed side by side, and from 1932 until his death in 1970 Antonio de Oliveira Salazar ruled the country as a right-wing dictatorship. His successors continued his policies, but in April 1974 a *coup* overthrew the government, and free elections were held a year later, bringing a Socialist government.

Terraced vineyards on the slopes of the Douro Valley, Portugal

Since the 1960's industrial development has been increasing fairly quickly, especially the production of steel and textiles. Some minerals are mined including tin, iron ores and copper. Recently the tourist industry has developed very rapidly, particularly in the Algarve province on the south coast.

Africa

MOROCCO
Kingdom
Area: 444,000 sq. km/171,000 sq. miles
Population: 16,300,000   Capital: Rabat
Flag: Red with five pointed green star

The narrow channel that leads from the Atlantic Ocean into the Mediterranean Sea is marked on each side by a rocky promontory: to the north is the Rock of Gibraltar, to the south, on the African coast, a similar landmark near the Spanish town of Ceuta. The ancients called these 'the Pillars of Hercules'. Today, Ceuta is merely a small foreign enclave within the large kingdom of Morocco.

Morocco contains two main mountain ranges – the Atlas Mountains and the Riff Mountains. The Riff rise up behind the coastline along the Mediterranean seaboard, while the Atlas Mountains run right through the centre of the country, dividing it into two fairly distinct regions. To the north of the mountains, especially on the coast, the land is partially sheltered from the hot winds of the Sahara, and there is a rainy season that may last from November to April. The mountain slops are often wooded. The southern slopes of the mountains, however, and the plains beyond are exposed to the dry Saharan winds, and are consequently desolate and unproductive. Here it is intensely hot in summer.

In the development of Morocco, the government is now mainly concerned with agriculture, mining, tourism and education. Dams are being constructed to conserve water for irrigation and to provide power for generating electricity. Morocco exports citrus fruits, many kinds of vegetables, skins and hides, and fish. The most important farm animals are sheep, goats and cattle, though donkeys, camels, horses and pigs are also to be found. The other main source of wealth in Morocco is mining. She produces phosphates, manganese, iron ore, lead and zinc, much of which is exported, as well as anthracite, petroleum, copper and tin. Though 70 per cent of the working population are still employed on the soil, Morocco is developing the industrial side of her economy. Food processing is an important part of this, and the country has one of the largest sardine canning industries in the world. Other manufactures include cement, construction materials, textiles, metallurgical processing, chemicals and fertilizers, agricultural equipment, petroleum production and sugar refining.

The history of Morocco is closely connected with the four Imperial cities of Fez, Marrakesh, Rabat and Meknes. The oldest of the Imperial cities is Fez, which was founded in AD 808 by Idriss II. The town was already well developed by the

Lush pasture surrounded by bare mountains is a feature of many regions in North Africa

An oasis near Marrakesh, Morocco. In the background are the Atlas Mountains

year 828, but when Idriss II died and the kingdom was divided up among his sons, disorders and anarchy ruined the work of the founders of the dynasty. In 1067, Fez fell into the hands of the first ruler of the Almoravid dynasty, Youssef Ben Tachfin. Scholars were attracted here from many parts of the world, and Fez became an Islamic capital. Under Almohades, the town was replanned, and their successors, the Merinides, who occupied Fez in 1248, saw the town pass through her greatest period, both as an artistic and as a spiritual centre. Fez lost pride of place as the capital city in the sixteenth century, but, even today, she still remains the intellectual capital of the country.

Marrakesh was founded nine centuries ago by the Almoravid, Youssef Ben Tachfin. His son built the first ramparts, parts of which remain still today, but most of the monuments that survive were erected under the Almohades and the Saadians. The latter are especially remembered for the fine tombs in which they are buried. But one of the greatest builders was Sidi Mohammed Ben Abdellah of the Alaouite dynasty who restored and decorated the pavilions in the Aguedal gardens, reorganized the Kasbah quarter and restored the Almohad mosque, also adding another mosque, the Berrima. One of the most attractive parts of Marrakesh is the Place Djemaa El Fna, the market place in the centre of the town where the small traders gather every morning; and where, in the evening, acrobats, story-tellers, snake charmers and dancers gather to entertain the crowd.

Rabat was originally a Roman settlement, but the history of the present town really dates back to the reign of Yacoub El Mansour, who died in 1199. He built the large enclosure that still surrounds the town today, and, inside the enclosure, started on what was to be one of the largest mosques in the world. Unfortunately, his death put an end to the work, and all that remains is Hassan's Tower, still an important feature of the skyline of Rabat. At the beginning of the seventeenth century, when Philip III of Spain expelled the last Moslems from his country, many of them came to settle in Rabat, and the fortunes of the town again improved. Rabat remains the winter capital of Morocco, while Tangier has comparatively recently been made the summer capital of the country.

The fourth of the Imperial cities is Meknes. The town is built around the stronghold erected by Youssef Ben Tachfin in 1063. The rulers of the Almohad dynasty built a network of canals to supply the town with water, while the Merinides added many new buildings. Under the Alaouites, a monumental enclosure was built, as well as mosques, the mellah, and several palaces of which remains can still be seen. But probably the most magnificent sight in the town is the walls and the triple bastions that surround it.

All four of these towns are on the northern side of the Atlas Mountains. To get a more balanced view of Morocco as a whole one should cross over the mountains and see the other side of the country. One of the roads climbs south through the Zad Pass, near the 3,737m (12,260-ft) peak at Djebel Ayachi, where snow may still lie in the early summer, through the 2,040m (6,700-ft) high Camel Pass, to Rich, on the Saharan side of the mountains. The road continues on down through the Zizi Valley, and soon the palm trees begin to appear, a winding strip of green along the valley floor, hedged in by the reddish rocks. As the valley widens and the surrounding hills become lower, the warm wind from the desert can be felt and the first dunes begin to appear. At last one reaches the oasis at Erfoud, in the region known as the Tafilalet. Near here are the ancient ruins of Sijilimassa, the origin of the Alaouite dynasty and once the terminus of the trans-desert caravans. In this area the kasbahs may be seen. These fortifications, with high, crenellated brick towers, look rather like the medieval castles of Europe. They are generally built on rocky promontories beside creeks or precipices, overlooking the old caravan routes that formed the main connections between the towns and villages.

ALGERIA
Republic
Area: 2,382,000 sq. km/920,000 sq. miles
Population: 15,800,000   Capital: Algiers
Flag: Green and white ground with red crescent and star

South-east of Morocco lies Algeria. The country has a long stretch of Mediterranean coast, and common frontiers with Mauretania, Mali, Niger, Libya and Tunisia as well as with Morocco. Although Algeria covers an area of 2·4 million sq. km (920,000 sq. miles) over 80 per cent of that is desert.

Algeria, too, is divided up by mountain ranges, though they are neither so well defined nor so high as those in Morocco. To the north are two chains of mountains, the Tellian Atlas (highest point, 2,318m (7,605 ft) and the Saharan Atlas. To the east, these two chains come together to form the massif that dominates the high plains of the Constantine area; while to the west they draw apart, giving place to a vast expanse of uneven, high

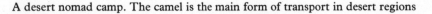

A desert nomad camp. The camel is the main form of transport in desert regions

plateaux furrowed by deep canyons. In these northern parts there is considerable variety in the land relief, but to the south, the surface of the Sahara is uniform and featureless over large distances. The main features are the vast sand dunes, some low mountains, and the occasional oasis. Only in the far south-west of the country is the monotony of the desert broken up by the Ahaggar Range, which reaches a height of 3,000m (9,840 ft). The Sahara is certainly the most arid and inhospitable of all the deserts in the world. Even the north-easterly trade winds that blow across it bring little rain, while they often create sandstorms.

The northern part of Algeria lies in the temperate zone and has a predominantly Mediterranean climate – cool, rainy winters and hot, dry summers. The temperature in Algiers, for example, varies between about 12 deg. C. in January and about 24 deg. C. in August. The extremes of the climate inland are here modified by the prevailing winds and by proximity to the coast. The interior of the country is in the dry, tropical zone, and here the contrast between the summer and winter climates is much greater. The winters are very severe, the summers torrid; it is much more difficult to live in this kind of climate than in a climate that is constantly hot or constantly cold. In the Constantine Plain, for example, the average January temperature is only 4 deg. or 5 deg. C., while the average maximum temperature in August is 34 deg. C. In the Sahara proper, the contrast is even more extreme – temperatures down to freezing point in winter and up above 50 deg. C. in summer. And it is not only with the seasons that these contrasts arise. The desert may be dazzlingly hot while the sun is still in the sky, but as soon as it sets the air quickly becomes cold.

As the rainfall is very irregular, it is not an easy job to produce crops in Algeria. Only the coastal areas have an adequate level of rainfall for cereal crops to be grown. On the Saharan Atlas and the high plateaux not only is the rainfall too low for crops, but the great contrast between summer and winter weather make both living and farming difficult. Often, it is difficult to make use of the rain that does fall. The soil, being dry and stony, cannot soak up the water, which merely flows away rapidly and is wasted.

It is said that Algeria once had extensive areas of

The Ahaggar Mountains in Algeria

forest. Today, only one per cent of the country is forested, and the Algerians are wisely trying to remedy this situation by replanting large areas.

Where the rainfall is fairly high, what forests there are are generally composed of Aleppo pines, thuyas and junipers. South of the coastal belt, trees are rare, and the only sort of vegetation that is at all extensive is alfa-grass. Palm trees, of course, may grow where there is water.

In spite of this barrenness, however, the Sahara is beginning to be put to some use by the Algerians. Oil, natural gas and iron ore have been found here in quantities, and the substantial oil and gas resources are now being exploited. The annual production of crude oil is now more than 50 million tonnes. The natural gas is piped to the coastal area, where, in the special plant built at Arzew, it is liquified. It can then be exported to Europe in specially designed tankers.

LIBYA
Republic
Area: 1,760,000 sq. km/679,000 sq. miles
Population: 2,200,000   Capital: Tripoli
Flag: Red, white and black horizontal stripes with gold emblem in centre

The neighbouring country of Libya also has large areas of the Sahara within its territory. It is, for the

Discoveries of great quantities of oil have made Libya and
other Arab countries very wealthy

most part, a place of sand and rock deserts. There are no permanent rivers in Libya, rainfall is intermittent, and, consequently, a good harvest is a rare thing. What cultivable land there is is found along the coastal strip in the north of Tripolitania and Cyrenaica, where cereal crops, nuts, olives, dates and citrus fruits are produced; and in the oases, where springs water a small fertile area in the barrenness of the desert. But, as in Algeria, the desert itself has now become a source of wealth. The state controls all matters to do with the oil industry, which produces over a hundred million tonnes of crude oil a year.

Formerly the desert was inhabited only by those who lived in the scattered oases and cultivated grain crops, dates and fruit; and by the nomads who moved with their tents and camels as the seasons dictated. Some of these nomads pass the summer near the Atlas Mountains, and the damper winter deep in the desert. They plant crops in the autumn which are ready to be harvested in the following spring when they return. Milk and meat are supplied by the animals they take with them – sheep and goats – which also make it essential for them to keep moving in search of adequate pastures. The slow plodding camel is the nomads' most valuable asset. He can live off the store of water and fat he keeps within his body for a considerable time, while continuing to carry the nomads and their equipment – the heavy woollen tents, their cooking pots, water-skins and other implements. The camel, too, can live off the tough, prickly plants of the desert, and, in the case of a sandstorm, can close his eyes, mouth and nose against the sand.

Oil, natural gas and iron ore are changing the pattern of life in the Sahara. New towns are springing up in the heart of the desert to supply the needs of the oil-men. Air-conditioned homes and shops have been built, power and water laid on, and facilities provided for contact with the outside world – roads and airfields. Arabs here can earn good, steady wages, and hope for a much higher standard of living than they ever enjoyed before.

EGYPT
Republic
Area: 1,000,000 sq. km/386,000 sq. miles
Population: 35,600,000   Capital: Cairo
Flag: Red, white and black horizontal bands with gold federal emblem in centre

Egypt (United Arab Republic) is in the north-east of Africa; the greater part of the country is desert; it has hardly any rainfall and depends entirely on the river Nile for its water. It is because of this situation that Egypt put so much faith and hard work into the construction of the Aswan Dam, completed in 1970, for not only does it increase by more than a quarter Egypt's agricultural land but provides much-needed hydro-electric power. Although Egypt is striving to develop industry she is still mainly an agricultural country; cotton is an important crop. Much money is earned from the tourist trade as Egypt is rich with historical remains.

Like Greece, Egypt had a great influence on western culture and it may be helpful to the reader to know something of its long history.

Egypt can trace back a continuous civilization to the year 4241 BC. It was in this year that Egypt adopted the calendar. There were about thirty dynasties, or lines of kings, between then and Alexander the Great who conquered Egypt. Egyptian culture reached a high peak during the IVth dynasty, 2900 BC, which is the age of the great pyramids. After Alexander's conquest the family of a Greek ruler named Ptolemy reigned in Egypt for two centuries. About 58 BC Rome began to gain control. Cleopatra, daughter of Ptolemy XI, tried, without success, to win back power for Egypt; she was the last independent sovereign of Egypt until the present century. Egypt remained under Rome for several centuries. Then the country was conquered by the Arabs. In 1798 Napoleon occupied Egypt but was defeated by Nelson outside Abukir in 1801. There then arose a remarkable Egyptian soldier named Mohamed Ali who was made pasha of Egypt by the Ottoman Sultan. He conquered the Sudan and introduced many reforms in Egypt. It was one of his descendants who was made King of Egypt as Fuad I, in 1922.

SUDAN
Republic
Area: 2,506,000 sq. km/967,000 sq. miles
Population: 16,900,000   Capital: Khartoum
Flag: Red, white and black horizontal bands with green triangle next to staff

The Sudan lies in the east of North Africa, south of Egypt. The boundary lies along the Red Sea in the east, where the chief port of the country Port Sudan is situated. To the north is the boundary with Egypt and to the south are Uganda and Lake Victoria. Kenya and Ethiopia are to the south east and Zaïre and the Republic of Chad to the west. Most of the country lies more than 300m (1,000 ft) above sea level; the White Nile runs from south to north from Uganda and the source in Lake Victoria to Egypt in the north. The Blue Nile flows into the country from Ethiopia, where it rises in Lake Tana. Both rivers flow through the Sudan and join at Khartoum, the capital in the centre of the country. At Atbara the Nile is joined by the river Atbara, and

flows out of the country at Wadi Haifa. The Nile plays a vital part in the economy of the country, providing the main source of water for the agriculture, which is the most important occupation for the population. The largest grain crop is millet, or *durn* as it is called, which forms the main source of food for the population. Sesame and ground nuts are also grown in sufficient quantities to be exported. However the main export crop is cotton. The Egyptian variety is grown primarily but the American cotton plant is also increasing. The Sudan is a major producer of Egyptian cotton. Most of the high quality cotton is produced on the government controlled scheme in Gezira with irrigation from the Sennar Dam on the Blue Nile.

The Sudan also produces 80 per cent of the world's gum arabic. Damming the Nile is providing an increasing quantity of water for irrigation and makes the extension of crops possible. In 1964 a dam at Kasham el Girba was completed, which provides irrigation for 120,000 hectares (300,000 acres) of land. Most of this land is being used as a resettlement area for the people displaced by the flooding around Wadi Haifa where the Egyptian

Cotton-picking in the Sudan

Rain clouds over the Sudan in the wet season

A large game reserve in Uganda

High Dam is being built on the Nile. The new dam at Roseires will provide irrigation for 1,200,000 hectares (3,000,000 acres) around the Blue Nile as well as being a vast resource of hydro-electricity.

The population of the Sudan is divided between Arabs and Africans and those of mixed descent. The northern tribes are mainly nomadic Arabs while the wetter southern provinces are inhabited by settled African tribes. Both depend heavily on livestock as a source of food where the irrigation schemes do not reach. The main means of communication is the railway. Steamer services go down to Juba from the railway which is connected with Nimule on the Uganda border by a bus service. The government airline provides internal and international services.

ETHIOPIA
Republic
Area: 1,222,000 sq. km/472,000 sq. miles
Population: 26,100,000
Capital: Addis Ababa
Flag: Green, yellow and red horizontal stripes with lion in centre

East of Sudan lies the wild mountainous country of Ethiopia (Abyssinia). This is an agricultural country producing such crops as maize, cotton, coffee, fruits and tobacco, and rearing livestock.

Ethiopia is one of the oldest Christian countries in the world, its ruling Hamitic people being followers of the Coptic Church. Legend has it that Menelik, the first King of Ethiopia, was the son of the Queen of Sheba and Solomon. In more recent

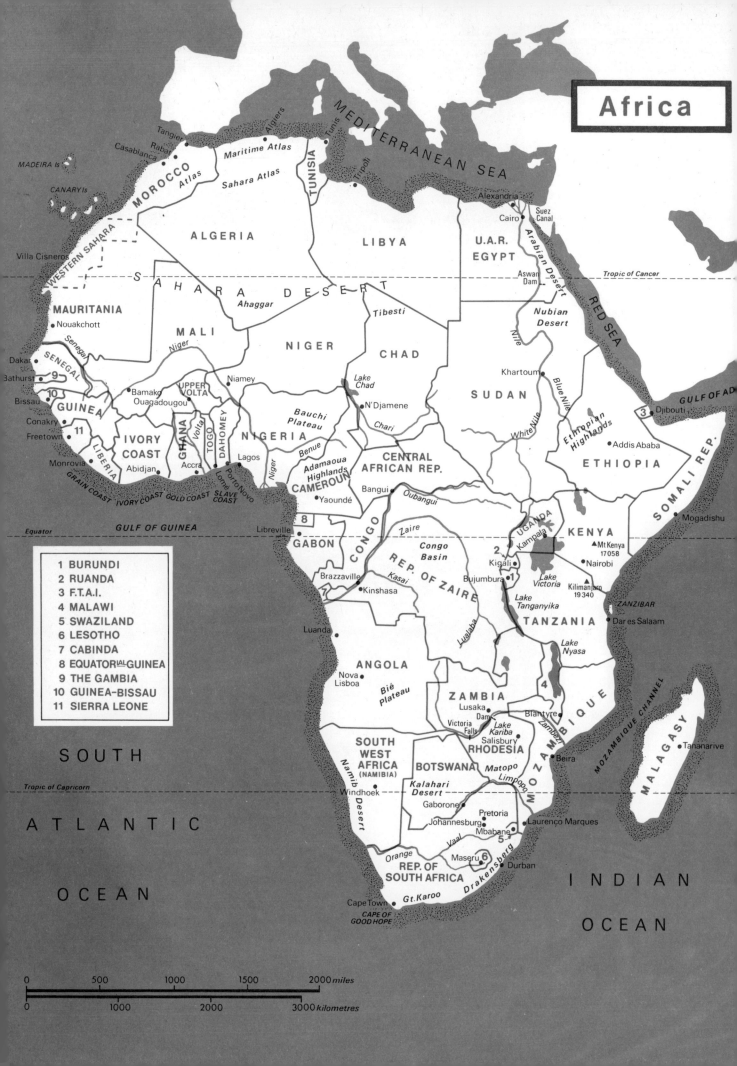

times Ethiopia has claimed the front pages of the world's press for in 1936 Mussolini not only invaded and conquered Ethiopia but used his airforce to bomb civilian populations whose only defence was a spear! In 1941 the Allies liberated Ethiopia and its King, Emperor Haile Selassie, returned to his country. He was overthrown in 1974 and died shortly afterwards.

GHANA
Republic in Commonwealth
Area: 238,500 sq. km/92,100 sq. miles
Population: 9,400,000   Capital: Accra
Flag: Red, yellow and green horizontal bands with black star in centre

Ghana, formerly the Gold Coast, lies to the west of Nigeria and, geographically and economically, is not too different from that country.

The climate of Ghana is particularly suited to the growing of cocoa and it supplies a large percentage of the world's need. There are good deposits of gold, bauxite, diamonds and manganese, all of which are exported. Tema Harbour is the largest artificial harbour in Africa and has done something to aid Ghana's prosperity. Round this new harbour are many industries, especially oil refining.

NIGERIA
Republic in Commonwealth
Area: 924,000 sq. km/357,000 sq. miles
Population: 79,800,000   Capital: Lagos
Flag: Green, white and green vertical bands

Nigeria is on the west coast of Africa, between four and fourteen degrees north of the equator. This means that its climate is what is known as 'equatorial'. It has two seasons, wet and dry, and the temperature is high all the year round. The rainy season lasts from April to October and the dry season from November to March. The temperature varies from the coast inland. On the coast it can be from 20 to 32 deg. C. but in the northern province, especially from October to April, it can sometimes be much hotter – often reaching 44 deg. C. The coldest the temperature ever gets is 10 deg. C. and

Nigerian women preparing the soil for the next crop. Women generally work in groups on the land; in this part of Africa one of the most important crops is the groundnut

135

A scene in a Nigerian village

Spinning cotton in an up-to-date factory in Nigeria

Fulani nomadic herdsmen live in an area stretching from Senegal in the west to Chad in the East

Harvesting in a banana plantation. The fruit, which is harvested when it is still green, is an important crop in many areas of Africa

that is only recorded at night. The climate is milder in the hill regions and the fluctuations of temperature far less extreme.

The river Niger divides Nigeria into three unequal parts. The river rises in the Futa Jalon Highlands on the borders with Sierra Leone and runs through Nigeria from north-west to south covering a distance of 1,175 km (730 miles). The Niger forms a delta where it reaches the coast and you can see on a map how it is slowly silting up and forming a promontory into the sea, where Port Harcourt is built. Deltas like these can be seen at the ends of many big rivers, and are formed from the mud and rubble that a river carries with it on its course. Sometimes they are very fertile but in Nigeria the whole coastline is covered with a mangrove swamp which cannot be used for farming because the thick roots of the mangroves are almost impossible to remove.

The other main river in Nigeria is the Benue, a tributary of the Niger which forms one of the arms of the river which divides the country. Its source is in the north-east in the Cameroon mountains and it runs for 800 km (495 miles) before joining the Niger at Lakoja. The delta formed by the Niger provides a useful system of inland waterways which provide cheap transport for goods. The coastal mangrove swamp varies from 15 to 100 km (10 to 60 miles) in width; north of this area is a region of tropical rain forest and oil palms; then the vegetation changes to savannah grasslands and woodland. North of the confluence of the Niger and the Benue at Lokoja the country rises to a high plateau at about 1,200m (4,000 ft) with some mountains as high as 1,800m (6,000 ft). Then the country slopes northwards towards the Sahara and becomes almost desert with Lake Chad to the north-east.

Oil is the primary source of the country's wealth, though about two-thirds of the working population is engaged in some form of agriculture, producing food and supplying large quantities to the urban areas. Great attention is being paid to the possibilities of increasing the yield of crops by far greater use of fertilizers and organic manures. On the plateau area there is a great deal of terraced agriculture and it is in this region that full use of organic waste as a fertilizer has been employed for many years to retain fertility in the soil and support a high density population. Some farmers still use a shifting method of agriculture which is wasteful of soil and involves using the full potential of the ground for a number of years and then leaving it. There are great dangers of erosion in this method and it means that land which could continue to be used can no longer be cultivated. Rotation of crops is used most in the region free from the tsetse fly where it is possible to keep cattle to graze on the land which is lying fallow. Nigeria is the world's largest exporter of groundnuts and the majority of of the crop comes from the north-west. The cotton crop is mainly the American variety.

The production of cocoa, coffee, soya beans and oil-palm products is increasing all the time and forms a very important part of the export market. Another factor in Nigerian agriculture is the great differences between the regions which make up the country. In particular the difference between the northern province and the sea coast provinces is very great; this means that there is a large domestic market for many of the crops grown in other regions of the country.

As in most African countries one of the major preoccupations of the farmers is the constant shortage of water. In Nigeria the great rivers are dammed to provide water to irrigate land that might otherwise be too dry to grow crops. The United Nations is working with the Nigerian government on a new scheme to irrigate a large area of land. In the northern provinces of Bornu and Kano investigations are being made to provide the kind of information necessary for the large-scale irrigation schemes. The engineers need to know about the kind of soil to be irrigated, the amount of water available, and the kind of crops to be grown before they can begin to plan for the huge dams necessary to store water for irrigation. In order to make more land available for farming the government is also encouraging soil conservation. This is necessary to prevent land from being exhausted through over-cultivation.

Another important development in Nigerian life is the exploitation of the vast fishing resources of Lake Chad. Before a start can be made on fishing the lake intensively an all-season road must be made which can withstand considerable amounts of water and hard weather and still preserve a surface good enough to take the heavy lorries which would be used for the transport of fish. Large sections of

Fulani cattle produce only a fraction of the milk yield of a European cow, as the grazing is so poor

the country suffer from this problem of isolation during the wet season when the normal, mud roads are turned into torrents of water in which any car rapidly becomes stuck. The weather is another factor which has prevented the exploitation of Lake Chad until now. There are frequent storms on the Lake and the papyrus rafts which the fishermen used for many years had to stay close to the shore to prevent being upset by one of these sudden storms. New boats are being introduced which can go out into the middle of the lake without danger and which are capable of carrying a catch of half a ton. It is impossible to tell what the full potential of the Lake is but it has been estimated that it is possible to catch one hundred thousand tons a year without any danger to the resources of the lake. The financial value of this new source of food is con-

siderable, but even more important, these vast quantities of fish will provide a high protein content in the Nigerian's daily diet which he lacks at the moment, especially in those areas where the tsetse fly prevent him from keeping cattle.

In northern Nigeria there is a large number of livestock in spite of the danger of disease from rinderpest and tsetse fly. Although most tropical diseases, both of humans and animals, are endemic, they are yielding to remedial and preventive measures. Sheep are being introduced in the north where a great deal of the land is well suited to them and attempts are being made to improve the two local breeds of sheep with the use of imported prize merino rams. Another animal which is very important in Nigerian farming is the Red Sokoto goat, which produces a fine skin used to make the

Conical huts used as storehouses for grain

delicate morocco leather. The skins are cured and dyed and used in the manufacture of many expensive luxury goods. Care is being taken to improve the breed and to extend its range all over the Province of Sokoto.

Forests are another important factor in the Nigerian economy. Until recently large areas of forest land have been cut and used with little attempt to replant or preserve the trees. As a result the wood resources of the country were seriously depleted and only careful conservation can replace what has been lost. There are now about $6\frac{1}{2}$ million hectares (16 million acres) of forest reserves where conservation is enforced, and many new trees are planted every year. There is a grave shortage of wood for building and firewood and new seedlings are being planted to make up the deficiency.

Lomé, in Nigeria, was the city in which an agreement was signed in 1975 between the EEC and 46 developing countries, covering overall trading and economic co-operation. The countries included the 18 which had originally signed treaties with the EEC at Yaoundé (see Cameroun) in 1963. The new countries were:

Congo People's Republic	Barbados★
Mauritius★	Bahamas★
Zaïre	Grenada
Kenya★	Guyana★
Tanzania★	Jamaica★
Uganda★	Trinidad & Tobago★
Botswana★	Fiji★
Gambia★	Tonga
Ghana★	Western Samoa
Lesotho★	Equatorial Guinea
Malawi	Ethiopia
Nigeria★	Guinea
Swaziland★	Guinea-Bissau
Sierra Leone★	Liberia
Zambia★	Sudan

★ indicates Commonwealth countries

CAMEROUN
Republic
Area: 475,000 sq. km/184,000 sq. miles
Population: 6,200,000   Capital: Yaoundé
Flag: Green, red and yellow vertical bands with two yellow stars on green band

Administered by Germany before the First World War, then by France as a League of Nations (later UN) trusteeship, the country became independent in 1960 as the Republic of Cameroun and joined with the former British trust territory of the Southern Cameroons.

The country has varied vegetation, from equatorial rain forest to savannah and desert scrub. Cattle and sheep are raised, together with cereals, cassava and sweet potatoes for local use. Exports are mainly timber, cocoa, palm products, bananas and coffee. Small quantities of gold, tin and titanium are mined.

At Yaoundé in 1963 a 5-year convention was signed between the EEC and 18 African states (ex-colonies) providing associate status for them. The states were:

Burundi	Mauretania
Cameroun	Niger
Central African Republic	Rwanda
Chad	Senegal
Dahomey (Benin)	Somalia
Gabon	Togo
Ivory Coast	Upper Volta
Mali	Congo (Brazzaville)
Malagasy Republic (Madagascar)	Congo (Leopoldville)

ZAÏRE
Republic
Area: 2,345,000 sq. km/905,000 sq. miles
Population: 23,600,000   Capital: Kinshasa
Flag: Green with emblem on yellow disc

Zaïre, formerly the Belgian Congo, is the largest country in Central Africa, its forests watered by the gigantic Zaïre river, which for part of its length separates Zaïre from the Congo People's Republic. Zaïre is truly a country of striking contrasts. Geographically it is part tropical forest and part savanna land. Economically the forests have produced very little save small quantities of wild rubber and elephant ivory. It has been – and still is – the natural home of such rare, shy creatures as the gorilla and okapi, the cousin of the giraffe. The forest is also the home of the pygmy whose life is not so different from that of the food hunters of prehistoric times. These people and their way of living are in striking contrast to the people of Kinshasa, the capital, who live in a modern city with all modern conveniences.

A large number of people still live in tribal communities, the men often working long distances away to keep their families in the villages. The main agricultural crops are palm oil, coffee and timber, most of which is exported. Zaïre is fortunate in being rich in minerals, especially copper from the province of Katanga, diamonds from Kasai and radium deposits near Lubumbashi. Independence from Belgium was granted in 1960, but there was much fighting between 1960 and 1964, when the country was declared a republic.

KENYA
Republic in Commonwealth
Area: 583,000 sq. km/225,000 sq. miles
Population: 12,500,000   Capital: Nairobi
Flag: Black, red and green horizontal bands divided by narrow white stripes with shield and crossed spears

Kenya, Tanzania's neighbour to the north, is also a young republic; in fact, its independence dates from 1963. Most of the population is black with a number of Indians and Europeans. Its situation economically is much the same as most of the newly formed states in East Africa, that is, agricultural production and light industry is gradually being established. Kenya's main crop is coffee but other crops such as tea and cotton are also grown. Nairobi is the capital and Mombasa the main seaport. The Nairobi National Park, a game reserve, is near the capital. On it can be seen a magnificent range of wildlife – lions, rhinoceroses, elephants, giraffes, zebras and many kinds of antelope.

TANZANIA
Republic in Commonwealth
Area: 940,000 sq. km/363,000 sq. miles
Population: 14,400,000
Capital: Dar es Salaam
Flag: Green and blue divided by black diagonal band edged with yellow

Tanzania is the republic formed early in 1964 when the old British colonies of Tanganyika and Zanzibar, both newly independent, formed a joint country of the island and the strip of land down the African coast. Most of Tanganyika is a large mountainous area of the Central African plateau from which rises Kilimanjaro, the highest mountain in Africa, 5,895m (19,340 ft) high. The Serengeti National Park, a famous wildlife reserve, is also within the borders of the country. Zanzibar is a small island, with a population of nearly 400,000. Its main

Mount Kilimanjaro in Tanzania, the highest mountain in Africa

importance lies in its production of a very large proportion of the world's supply of certain spices, notably cloves and clove oil. In both countries the production of food for domestic use and export is the primary occupation. The main commercial crops are cotton, coffee, oil seeds and sisal and all these are exported in large quantities. A certain amount of minerals is mined, the most important of which are diamonds, gold, lead and mica. The majority of Tanzanian industries are involved in processing the goods produced in the country, leather working of many kinds is particularly important, and shoes are made from the high quality leather that the cattle herds of Tanganyika produce. Zanzibar also grows and processes coconuts, coconut oil and copra. The problem of language in a newly formed nation has been solved by making Swahili, the predominent language, the official language and having English as a second official language, which can be used both in schools and universities and by government officials. The main towns of Tanzania are along the coast of the Indian Ocean where the capital Dar-es-Salaam is situated. The capital of the island is the city of Zanzibar.

ZAMBIA
Republic in Commonwealth
Area: 753,000 sq. km/291,000 sq. miles
Population: 4,600,000   Capital: Lusaka
Flag: Green with vertical bands of red, black and orange beneath gold eagle
To the south-west of Tanzania is Zambia which until its independence in 1963 was known as Northern Rhodesia. Like Rhodesia (see below) it is an agricultural country but is also very rich in copper ore, its main and most valuable export. On the eastern border of Zambia is Malawi, one of the smallest independent states in Africa, and a member of the Commonwealth. The mainstay of the country is agriculture and its principal crops are cotton, tea and tobacco, much of which it exports.

RHODESIA
Republic
Area: 389,000 sq. km/150,000 sq. miles
Population: 5,900,000   Capital: Salisbury
Flag: Green, white and green vertical bands with shield on white band

Rhodesia covers the area originally known as Matabeleland, Mashonaland and Manicaland south of the Zambesi river. The territory was named after Cecil Rhodes who first encouraged settlement of the centre of Africa. The land is predominantly agricultural with many large farms and ranches. One of the most important crops is the tobacco crop of which large quantities are sent to Europe. There are about 270,000 European settlers in Rhodesia, mainly owning farms or working in offices in Salisbury or Bulawayo, the two largest towns. The African population numbers nearly six million and they mainly work on the farms. An equal area of land is allotted to the European and African communities, with a further 6½ million acres designated as a National Area. Rhodesia is completely surrounded by land. Zambia and Angola lie to the north and west of the country, Mozambique to the east, and the provinces of South Africa, Natal and Bechuanaland to the south. In addition to tobacco many other agricultural products are produced for export but Rhodesia is very dependent on external supplies for minerals and oil.

In 1965 Rhodesia, under its Premier, Ian Smith, made a unilateral declaration of independence (UDI) and broke away completely from Great Britain and the Commonwealth, who were pressing for faster progress to be made towards greater representation of the black Rhodesians in the government of the country. Trade sanctions were at that time imposed on Rhodesia by the United Nations and caused considerable economic difficulty. Widespread support for Rhodesian African Nationalist parties, together with opposition from African states to the Smith regime, has threatened the security of the white-dominated government.

SOUTH AFRICA
Republic
Area: 1,221,000 sq. km/471,000 sq. miles
Population: 23,700,000   Capital: Pretoria
Flag: Orange, white, blue horizontal stripes with three small flags imposed
If you look on the map you can see that South Africa is a very large country, including many mountains and rivers within its boundaries. There are the southern ranges around the Table Mountain and the great range of the Drakensbergs in the east of the country. The high land in the centre is

Part of the Victoria Falls, Rhodesia, on the border with Zambia

An African village in the Transkei, South Africa. The round, thatched houses are whitewashed in different patterns

143

An African township outside Johannesburg

A highly mechanized orange farm on the Sunday River, South Africa. The tractor is making irrigation channels to bring water to the trees

excellent grazing land and there are the richest farmlands and mineral resources anywhere in Africa. In the south are a series of mountain ranges rising to a wide plateau and to the north are more fertile plains for pasture. Natal in the east is the most fertile of all, running along the coastline.

The original wealth of South Africa was and still is based on her rich mineral resources. The country contains large gold mines producing large quantities yearly. There are also diamond, coal, copper and silver mines and tin and asbestos are important. A country with such resources would be rich without farming land as well but the produce of South African farms is almost as great as the mineral wealth. All kinds of crops are grown, the most important being wheat, maize, barley and oats, all

Planting out rice in a paddy field in the Malagasy Republic

of which are exported in large quantities. Wool and groundnuts are also important.

The South Africa countryside is very beautiful. It includes many large game reserves which are kept in good condition for the benefit of the tourists South Africa attracts. It has also large beaches and holiday resorts. South Africa for most of her history was a colony and like most colonies a proportion of the population is descended from immigrants from overseas, particularly from European countries and Asia. However in South Africa the African population is much larger than the white population. There are approximately fifteen million Bantus and other African tribes living within the borders of South Africa and about four million white South Africans as well as a number of Asians and the 'coloureds' who are of mixed black and white descent. It is South African policy to try to keep black and white populations separate as far

as possible, though this is made difficult by the necessity of using a large black labour force to keep industry going. African 'homelands' called Bantustans have been set aside for the blacks and given a limited amount of power to run their own affairs. Recently South Africa has been entering into discussions and negotiations with neighbouring black African states. The original inhabitants, the Bushmen and Hottentots, have now dwindled to a mere few thousand.

MALAGASY REPUBLIC
Republic
Area: 587,000 sq. km/227,000 sq. miles
Population: 7,700,000 Capital: Tananarive
Flag: Red and green horizontal bands with vertical band of white at left
The Malagasy Republic is the country on the island known as Madagascar, in the Indian Ocean 400 km

(250 miles) from the south-east coast of Africa. It has three main geographical areas, a hot, wet, coastal strip where the rainfall can be as much as 280 cm (110 in) a year. The central highlands are a forest covered mountainous area where the temperature ranges are extreme, but the rainfall is lower than on the coast. The western area is much hotter than the east coast and has marked wet and dry seasons with a far lower rainfall. Most of the people are occupied in some form of agriculture which is the main industry of the island. The coastal region is the main farmland and a large number of different crops are produced. Along the east coast the spices that first attracted European colonizers are still grown, especially cloves and vanilla. Coffee is another important crop on the coast while in the highlands cattle and horses are bred. The island's most important mineral is graphite which is used in the electronics industry but mica and uranium are also exported.

Union of Soviet Socialist Republics

USSR
Republic
Area: 22,400 sq. km/8,650,000 sq. miles
Population: 248,600,000   Capital: Moscow
Flag: Red ground with five-pointed star above hammer and sickle

The first Russian dynasty was founded at Novgorod, near present-day Leningrad, in AD 862. The founder was Rurik, a Norse war-leader, who took over Novgorod, not by battle, however, but by invitation. The Slavs who lived in this area wanted some order to be imposed on their land. Rurik was willing to oblige, and his cousin Oleg, who succeeded him, expanded the kingdom southwards, taking the already important city of Kiev in the Ukraine. Through Kiev, Russia was influenced by

Byzantium, the last dazzling remnant of the shrunken Roman Empire – she accepted the Greek Orthodox faith, the Cyrillic alphabet, and much of Byzantine art and culture.

In 1237 began the Mongol, or Tartar, conquest. This fierce and warlike people, led by a nephew of Genghis Khan, destroyed and occupied the southern part of Russia which Kiev had dominated, setting up their own capital at Sarai, on the Volga. They were content merely to plunder and raid northern Russia. This was a difficult period for the Russian rulers, who had not only the cruel attacks of the Mongols to fear from the south, but also the ambitions of the Swedish rulers to the north and of the Teutonic Knights to the west. It is recorded that the Russians fought these German Knights on

An open-air market in Tashkent, the capital of the Uzbek S.S.R.

The Moscow skyline with the Kremlin on the left

the frozen surface of Lake Peipus, and that the Germans were so heavily armed that the ice gave way and they were drowned.

The long period of Tartar rule only came to an end during the reign of Ivan the Great (1462–1505), who at last managed to instil a sense of nationhood in his people. Ceremony at this time became an important part of Russian kingship, largely because Ivan married Sophia Paleologue, niece of the last Greek Emperor of Constantinople, and brought not only her to Moscow, but also much of the ceremonial of the Byzantine court, even adopting their symbol, the Byzantine double-eagle, as his own. Sophia summoned some Italian architects to Moscow to design the Kremlin. Ivan called himself Czar, or Caesar.

His grandson, Ivan the Terrible, also called himself Czar, but he added on the title 'Autocrat' too. His reign proceeded in a style well-suited to his titles. The absolute power of the monarchy was the keystone of his policy, and he introduced secret police, the better to enforce his authority. He extended the boundaries of Russia towards the south-east, capturing Kazan and Astrakhan in the region of the Caspian Sea. Towards the end of his life his conscience became too heavy for him, and he entered a monastery.

The Romanovs, whose line was founded in 1613 by Michael Romanov, a grand-nephew of Ivan the Terrible, established the familiar backcloth to the events of Russian history which was to remain virtually unchanged until the October Revolution in 1917 – the absolute separation of the privileged part of society from the peasantry, who were for-

bidden to travel between one part of the country and another, or to work for landlords other than their own, while the noblemen grew rich on their work. The process was accelerated under the remarkable Peter the Great (1672–1725), a man who, like many before and after him on the Russian throne, was at times revoltingly cruel, but whose personal talents were considerable. The main feature of his reign was that he brought Russia out of her isolation from the rest of Europe. By defeating Charles of Sweden in 1709 he at last secured for Russia a point of access to the high seas in the Baltic. He founded the Russian Navy and was himself the first Russian monarch to travel abroad. Moscow ceased to be the capital of Russia, and was eclipsed by a new town built on the marshes near the Baltic Sea, called St. Petersburg. It developed into a fine eighteenth-century city, built on more than 100 islands, with a vast network of canals and more than 400 bridges. In 1914 it was renamed Petrograd, and, after the Revolution, became Leningrad. Here the Russian monarchy played out the last 200 years of its violent and extravagant career.

Catherine the Great (1762–96) was a German and had no Russian blood in her at all. She became Empress by marrying the Grand Duke Peter, later Peter III, who was soon deposed and murdered. Catherine herself was a cultured person who wrote poetry and plays and corresponded with Voltaire and Frederick the Great; but she was no less absolutist than her predecessors. Disgruntled serfs (and some members of the upper classes who sympathized with them) were savagely put down.

Red Square in Moscow, where Russia stages her great parades, adjoins the Kremlin, an old fortress which has for long been the heart of Russia's life and the seat of government. Lenin's Tomb is on one side of Red Square

Catherine probably hated nobody more than the French and American Revolutionaries. She would willingly have had the British employ Russian mercenaries against the Americans. At home, the nobility were awarded greater and greater privileges. Catherine also continued the territorial expansion of Russia, which, by the end of her reign, included the lands near the Black Sea and the Caucasus.

During the nineteenth century, signs of change began at last to appear; not among the czars, how-ever, who perpetuated the habits of repression and incompetence that had been the hallmark of their predecessors. The educated people, though, and many of the aristocracy among them, began to see that the Russian way of life would no longer do, while remaining incapable of finding a viable alternative. Socialism, nihilism, anarchism – all had their following. A means of peaceful reform might perhaps have been found with the co-operation of Alexander II (1855–81), who secured the emancipation of the serfs and planned further reforms; but

G.U.M., a large department store in Moscow

The Cathedral of St Basil faces Lenin's Tomb in Red Square. It is one of the most ornate and colourful ecclesiastical buildings in the world. It was started by Ivan the Terrible in 1554, but after the Revolution in 1917 it ceased to be used for religious purposes and was converted into an historical museum

Odessa on the Black Sea in the southern Ukraine is important for shipbuilding and as a large wheat-exporting port

he was assassinated, and his successor returned to the pattern of his ancestors.

Revolution in Russia came in three phases, the first after their defeat in the War with the Japanese in 1905. The result of this was that, for the first time in Russian history, some elements of representative government were introduced through the inauguration of the Duma, or parliament; but important laws could still not be changed without the consent of the Czar. The Czar himself, the unimaginative and weak Nicholas II (1894–1917., rapidly lost the popularity he had once possessed when his troops massacred a procession of workers in St. Petersburg. The leaders of the underground revolutionary movements, like Lenin, head of the Bolsheviks, were not to be satisfied with the small concessions of 1905.

In 1917, as Russian troops died in large numbers on the German front and as the government broke down at home, dissatisfaction came to a head and resulted in the 'February' Revolution. Czarist troops refused to put down strikers in Petrograd, and the Duma declined to dissolve itself in spite of the commands of the Czar. Instead, it established a provisional government under Alexander Kerensky. The Czar abdicated, and the rule of the Romanovs was never revived. This revolution had been almost bloodless, and was succeeded towards the end of the year by another revolution, also virtually bloodless, but of far greater importance than the 'February' Revolution. This was the 'October' Revolution, and victory came to the Bolsheviks and their leader Lenin. The factories, the land and the banks were all taken over by the State. The object was to set up a fully socialist state.

This object was not to be achieved so easily. The Great Powers of the time threw up their hands in horror at the idea of the Bolsheviks ruling Russia. The United States, Britain, France, Poland, Japan and other foreign countries all sent troops into Russia, and the country was torn apart by civil war between the 'Whites' and the 'Reds'. It was not until 1920 that the conflict ended in victory for the 'Reds'.

The USSR today is a vast and highly developed country stretching from the Arctic Ocean to the Caspian, and from the Baltic to the Pacific, occupying more than 6 per cent of the earth's inhabited surface. There are numerous mountain ranges

Many people in the southern republics of the U.S.S.R. still wear national costumes and follow their traditional way of life

Icefloes in the arctic regions of Siberia in northern Russia

along the southern and eastern borders of the country – the Carpathians, which run through Poland, Romania and the Ukraine; the Caucasus Mountains between the Caspian and the Black Sea in Georgia; and the mountains of Siberia. The barrier of the Ural Mountains divides European Russia from the less populated areas of Asian Russia. Many different races occupy this area, the most important being the Russians themselves,

A cattle-breeding farm on the steppes. The row of trees has been planted to form a windbreak

Yalta, a popular holiday resort on the Black Sea

A mechanized bottling plant

Herding sheep on a collective farm in the southern U.S.S.R.

Ukrainians, Byelorussians, Uzbeks, Kazakhs, Azerbaidjanianis, Armenians, Georgians and Lithuanians.

Since the Revolution, the USSR has been transformed from being a primarily agricultural country, in which the dominating group was that of the small peasant farmer, into one of the greatest industrial powers in the world. The industrialization and urbanization of Russia has progressed even more rapidly since the Second World War. At the beginning of that war, 32 per cent of the population lived in towns, while today more than 50 per cent of the people are town dwellers. The output of some of the Russian industries is immense – 128 million tonnes of steel, 402 million tonnes of crude oil, 730,000 motor-cars in one year. The Soviet Union has also made fantastic advances in science, especially space exploration and atomic power. Her aircraft industry is equally advanced both commercially and militarily.

Progress in agriculture has also been considerable, though not as great as many Russians had

Large-scale wheat farming on the steppes

hoped. Farming has recently suffered a number of set-backs due partly to the way in which the collective farms are organized, and partly to droughts, and consequently grain has had to be purchased from countries like Canada and the United States. New plans have been adopted to give greater incentives to the farmers to obtain a bigger yield, without abandoning the idea of the collective farm. Better results are especially needed where livestock is concerned. New lands – called the Virgin Lands – have been put under the plough in the east of the country and have added vastly to the acreage available for grain, though some of the soil has turned out to be unsuitable for cultivation because of erosion and has had to be abandoned. Nearly two-fifths of the Soviet Union is covered by forest, which is a source of great wealth to the Russians.

The most important of the fifteen Republics is the Russian Soviet Federal Socialist Republic, whose capital is Moscow. It occupies 78 per cent of the total area of the USSR. The two largest industrial centres in the country, Moscow and Leningrad, are contained within it. The RSFSR produces most of the Soviet oil output, and is also important in the production of iron and steel and in engineering; most of the Russian grain crop is produced here on the steppes and on the western Siberian plain, to the east of the Urals.

The Ukraine, the second largest Republic in population, lies between the RSFSR and the Black Sea, and in its southern part is the main centre of Russian coal-mining and of the iron and steel industry. The Ukraine is to the USSR what the Ruhr is to Germany. Engineering and chemical industries are well established here, and it is the main sugar-producing area. Coal, iron ore, salt and manganese are mined.

Byelorussia, one of the most backward areas in Europe at the beginning of this century, lies in the western part of European Russia, and its capital is at Minsk. Its greatest disadvantage was the many areas of swamp, but these have now been drained, and the agriculture of the area is greatly improved as a result. Engineering and woodworking are the chief industries.

Georgia, lying on the borders of Turkey and Iran, has a very different climate from most of the USSR. On the shores of the Black Sea, the climate is sub-tropical. Grapes and tobacco are the chief agricultural products, but there are also useful mineral deposits, notably of oil, manganese and coal.

Uzbekistan consists, for the most part, of great waterless deserts. The population is centred in the few large oases which are the only habitable parts of the Republic. These include Tashkent, Samar-

Houses and farm buildings on
a Soviet collective farm

kand and Bokhara, the ancient cities which were important trading points in medieval times. Most of the Soviet cotton is grown in Uzbekistan, and considerable efforts have been made to improve the irrigation of the area and so increase production, including the building of the Great Ferghana Canal.

Kazakhstan, the second largest Republic in the Union, is a place of steppes and arid deserts, with a dry continental climate. Nevertheless, there is a great deal of stock-raising here, and also grain growing. Many 'virgin lands' have been turned over to cultivation, though they depend heavily on favourable weather which is not always forthcoming. Cotton is grown in southern Kazakhstan. There are important deposits of coal, oil and copper, and the metal industry has been developed.

The remaining Republics of the Soviet Union are those of Azerbaidjan, Lithuania, Moldavia, Latvia, Estonia, Kirghizia, Tadzhikistan, Turkmenistan and Armenia.

Asia

TURKEY
Republic
Area: 780,600 sq. km/301,300 sq. miles
Population: 37,400,000   Capital: Ankara
Flag: Red ground with white crescent and star
The mainland of Turkey occupies the land separating the Black Sea from the Mediterranean. The country has parts both in Europe and in Asia. Its land encloses the Sea of Marmara and the entry to the Black Sea through the Bosphorus and the Dardanelles. Until this century access to the Black Sea was a source of constant friction between the powers of Europe and Russia and the position of Turkey was constantly under dispute while the favour of the ruler of Turkey, the Sultan, was sought by both sides. Since 1923 Turkey has been developing as a modern state. After the First World War the Sultan was deposed and a republic set up by Kemal Atatürk and a large programme of modernization was begun. Turkey now has several modern cities, Ankara, the capital, having a population of nearly 1½ million.

The main activity in Turkey is agriculture in which two-thirds of the working population take part and which accounts for over 60 per cent of Turkey's external trade. The second most important occupation is the exploitation of Turkey's considerable mineral wealth, especially coal; new consumer industries are also being developed.

ISRAEL
Republic
Area: 20,700 sq. km/7,990 sq. miles
Population: 3,200,000   Capital: Jerusalem
Flag: White with two horizontal blue stripes, shield of David in centre
The state of Israel was set up after the Second World War to provide a national home for members of the Jewish faith. It occupies an area of fertile land along the coast of the Mediterranean where intensive agriculture is the main activity. The famous Jaffa orange is grown in large quantities, mainly for export, and citrus fruits form a very high proportion of the produce of the country. Various industries are being established, among them textiles, clothes and light engineering. Diamonds are also polished in large quantities and form a major export to Europe and America. The limiting factor in the production of crops is the shortage of water. The climate is very hot, especially during the summer, and extensive irrigation has to be used to achieve as much cultivation as possible.

SYRIA
Republic
Area: 185,200 sq. km/71,500 sq. miles
Population: 6,900,000   Capital: Damascus
Flag: Red, white and black horizontal bands with gold federal emblem in centre
Syria is mainly a Moslem country, rich in historical remains. Damascus has been a city continuously for over 4,000 years. It was under French mandate, but became a republic during the Second World War. Mainly agricultural, it produces wheat, barley and cotton. Oil has also been discovered.

Syria, like Jordan and Lebanon, has the problem of finding sufficient water to irrigate crops and produce more food though modern technology is helping to overcome this difficulty to some extent. All three countries are largely agricultural, though Jordan exports phosphates from the Dead Sea and Lebanon, famed for its cedar trees (a cedar tree is on the national flag) exports quantities of fruit.

IRAQ
Republic
Area: 434,000 sq. km/168,000 sq. miles
Population: 10,400,000   Capital: Baghdad
Flag: Red, white and black horizontal stripes with three green stars on white stripe

A kibbutz on the edge of the Negev Desert, Israel, where the use of modern methods of farming and irrigation have much increased the crop yields

Iraq, once known as Mesopotamia, is the land between the two rivers Euphrates and Tigris and was the land of two ancient civilizations, Babylonia and Assyria. The main activity of the people is agriculture and its chief crops are cereals, dates, fruits and cotton, a great deal of which is exported. Iraq's principal source of wealth is its oil. The capital is Baghdad which in ancient times was on the trade route between Persia (Iran) and India. Haroun Al-Rashid, one of the characters in *The Arabian Nights*, greatly enlarged the city in the ninth century. Now it is a busy commercial centre – and most of Iraq's industries are located there.

A confederation of the oil-producing countries (OPEC) was formed to decide on a common policy for the production and export of petroleum products. The decision to raise the price of oil in 1974 was one of the factors leading to worldwide inflation, as it increased the cost of transport, electricity and consequently of nearly all consumer goods.

SAUDI ARABIA
Kingdom
Area: 2,264,000 sq. km/874,000 sq. miles
Population: 8,400,000 Capital: Riyadh
Flag: Green oblong with Arabic lettering above white scimitar

Saudi Arabia occupies most of the Arabian Peninsula and is very rich in oil, its principal export. Its agriculture is very much the same as the other Middle East countries in produce and physical conditions. Saudi Arabia has two capitals, Riyadh and Jeddah. Mecca is the oldest city in Arabia and the birthplace of Mohammad, the founder of Islam. Every year over six hundred thousand pilgrims visit Mecca. The object of the pilgrimage is the Mosque of Mecca, particularly the Kaaba (a cube) and the Black Stone inset in it. The pilgrims walk round the Kaaba seven times, kiss the Black Stone and touch another stone on the south side.

156

IRAN
Empire
Area: 1,650,000 sq. km/636,000 sq. miles
Population: 31,300,000   Capital: Tehran
Flag: Green, white and red stripes with lion and sun in centre

Iran (Persia) is one of the most ancient countries in the world. In the sixth century BC the Persians, a nomadic tribe, settled in the country and joined with the Medes in overthrowing the Assyrian Empire. Under Cyrus II, or the Great, the Persians captured the Medean capital, and in a very short time they had greatly extended their empire which under Darius I reached its greatest extent. When Alexander the Great rose to power in Greece the Persians were defeated at the Battle of the Hellespont in 334 BC.

In AD 642 Persia came under Arab rule and was converted to Islam. During this period Persian art and science flourished. In 1037 Seljuk Turks from the Turkmen steppes ruled the country. Twenty years later Genghiz Khan and his Mongols arrived, and spread destruction through North Persia. For a period Persia was ruled by Hulagu, the grandson of Genghiz Khan, and he founded a Mongol kingdom in Persia. In the sixteenth century a new line of Persian kings arose, the chief of whom was Abbas the Great. He defeated the Ottoman Turks and with English aid drove the Portuguese from Hormuz.

During the First World War Persia was occupied for a short time by both Britain and Russia. In 1921 an army officer named Reza Khan led a revolution, and in 1925 was elected Shah or king. During the Second World War both Britain and Russia accused Persia of favouring Germany, and again they occupied the country and forced Reza Khan to abdicate in favour of his son, Mohammed Reza Pahlavi.

Iran is essentially an agricultural country, 75 per cent of the working adults being engaged in agriculture. Like most countries of the Middle East the Iranian people working on the land have a very low living standard. In recent years the Shah of Iran has introduced many land reforms to improve the lot of the people; in fact, he delayed his official coronation until he had achieved this. The main crops are wheat, cotton, rice, sugar-beet, vegetables and fruits. The chief export is, of course, petroleum and over 2,000 million barrels are shipped annually.

The income derived from oil has resulted in Iran becoming a donor of aid to developing countries instead of, as formerly, receiving aid herself. The only other significant export is carpets.

INDIA
Republic in Commonwealth
Area: 3,268,000 sq. km/1,262,000 sq. miles
Population: 563,500,000   Capital: Delhi
Flag: Tricolour of saffron, white, dark green with wheel in blue in centre of white band

India is one of the largest countries in the world. Its northern boundary is marked by the great mountain chain of the Himalayas. To the west is the Arabian Sea, to the east the Bay of Bengal. From Cape Comorin, the southernmost tip of India, it is 3,200 km (2,000 miles) to the country's northernmost boundary.

Some of the largest rivers in Asia flow across India. The Ganges begins as a small trickle from an icy cave 4,000m (13,000 ft) up in the Himalayas. By the time it reaches the plain below (the plain which separates the chain of the Himalayas from the Deccan Plateau which occupies the greater part of central and southern India) it is already a great river. Flowing on through the states of Uttar Pradesh and Bihar it gathers to it the waters of other large rivers – the Yamuna, the Gumti, the Gagra, the Sarda, the Gandak, the Sone and the Kosi. Like the other rivers which flow from the Himalayas, the Ganges brings down with it heavy loads of sand, gravel and silt which it deposits on its bed, thereby raising the water-level above that of the surrounding countryside. In times of heavy rain, this means that flooding is inevitable, and during the monsoon (June to September) the people go in constant fear of the water ruining their property. As it nears the sea, the Ganges begins to split up into several branches, some of which cross into Bangladesh before they reach the coast at the mouths of the Ganges. On one of these branches lies Calcutta, the chief city of West Bengal, which is an important trade centre in the fertile area of the Ganges plain. Altogether, the Ganges is 2,494 km (1,550 miles) long.

The rivers on the Deccan Plateau are very different from those which originate in the Himalayas. For most of the year they are merely trickles in beds of stone or sand. Only during the four

Bombay, one of the largest cities and seaports in India, is built on an island

months of the monsoon do they really become worthy of the name river. Generally, their beds are deep enough to carry the monsoon rains, so there is no fear of flooding. This short and valuable supply of water has to be carefully used so that it will last for the whole year. Dams have been built across these rivers to store up the water, and canals lead the water from the reservoirs to the fields.

Another great river is the Sindhu, or Indus, whose source is in Tibet. For most of its length it flows through Pakistan.

The river Sindhu gave rise to the words 'Ind' and 'Hind', names applied to 'the land beyond the Indus'. From these words we get 'India' and 'Hindu'. The Dravidians, the original inhabitants of India, were a primitive people, whose religion was based on the worship of nature gods. In about 2,000 BC, India was invaded by the Arians, a tall, fair people from the North who imposed their way of life upon the Dravidians. One of the effects of this was that the religion of the Arians, which is described in an ancient book known as the *Rig-Veda*, was mingled with the Dravidians' religion. The result, which is in part a religion and in part a social system, we call Hinduism. As a religion it is very tolerant, respecting the faiths outside Hinduism and never seeking converts. Hinduism may mean different things to different people, for it includes the worship of a number of gods and many different beliefs are adhered to. Hindus believe that appreciation of beauty and respect and regard for women are an important part of their religion. As a social system, Hinduism divided people into superior and inferior groups known as 'castes'. In order of precedence these were: priests (Brahmins), soldiers, merchants, and labourers or artisans. At the very bottom come the pariahs or 'untouchables'. Recently this caste system has been much modified. The Indian Constitution forbids discrimination on grounds of race, religion, creed or sex, the untouch-

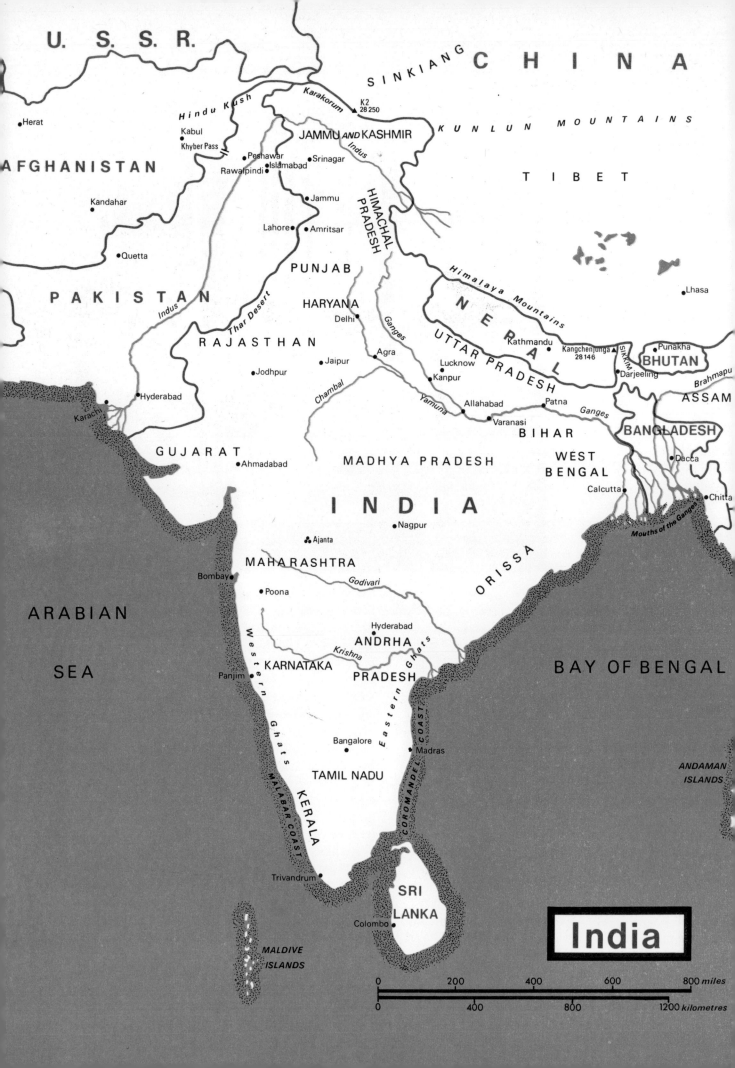

The Taj Mahal at Agra, India. This beautiful example of Moslem architecture was built about 1630 by Shah Jehan, in memory of his wife, Mumtaz Mahal

able caste has been abolished, and discrimination on these grounds has been made a criminal offence.

In the fifth century BC the Hindu religion had become excessively formalized and ritualistic, and, out of the reaction against this, developed Buddhism. Prince Siddharta Gautama, the Buddha, was the son of a king in north-east India, who left his palace to become a hermit and to discover why the world was such a sorrowful place. Ritual and ceremony he abandoned and superstition had no place in his faith. He taught his disciples to accept that the world would always be an unhappy place and that they should learn to forget themselves through meditation and self-discipline. Today it is still an important characteristic of a good Buddhist to renounce pleasure and reward for himself while being kind and generous to others. Though there are still Buddhists in India, it is in Asia that the faith is most widespread.

There are two other religions native to India: Jainism and Sikhism. Mehavir, the founder of Jainism, lived a little earlier than Buddha, but he also revolted against contemporary Hinduism. He taught that no living thing should be injured and believed that plants, birds and all kinds of animals should be treated with respect and consideration. The Jains shun wealth and possessions, though their temples are among the most beautiful in India, and they teach peace and non-violence. The Sikhs are a religious sect founded in the fifteenth century by Guru Nanak (1469–1539) who rejected the divisions of caste and the worship of idols and taught his followers to believe in simplicity and equality. By the beginning of the eighteenth century the Sikhs had become a nation of warriors settled mainly in the Punjab which they defended fiercely against the British in 1839. The Punjab nevertheless became part of the Empire in 1849.

A tea plantation in hilly country

Islam (the religion of Mohammed) has had an important influence on the history of India. It was brought to India in the seventeenth century by Arab traders and seafarers. One of the greatest of the Moghul Emperors was the Emperor Akbar, a Muslim, as one who practises Islam is called, who believed strongly in religious tolerance. He himself married a Hindu princess and gave Hindus important posts at court. He sought to get the best out of both religions, and, as a result, architecture, art and philosophy flourished during his reign.

India today is primarily an agricultural country. Over 70 per cent of their people make their living by working the land. Most of the area used for crops is taken up by food grains. The chief cereal, and the staple food of eastern and southern India, is rice, while wheat, the staple food of northern India, comes next in importance. Maize, barley and millet are also of importance. India is the biggest producer of tea and peanuts in the world, and the second largest producer of rice, jute and raw sugar.

Agriculture faces very considerable problems. Because so many people are dependent on it for their living, it is a far greater catastrophe when the harvest fails than it would be in Europe, for example. Small farmers are still very much dependent on the weather, and a prolonged drought can quickly result in widespread famine.

Dams and canals have been constructed to save as much water as possible and to assure its distribution in times of drought. Projects are in operation for improving the life of the small farmer, both on the land and in his village. Through these projects, land is reclaimed, fertilizers provided, water supplies are improved, as is the quality of the seeds and implements used by the farmers. Better facilities are provided for education, public health and medical attention, and new housing projects are initiated.

Each village is for many purposes a self-govern-

The men in red shirts are the porters at this Indian railway station

In India the water buffalo has been domesticated and is a gentle creature. It is principally used for pulling ploughs and carts, but also provides milk

ing unit. The council of village elders has charge of all the development projects in the area – plans to make agriculture more productive, reorganization of the labour force in the village so as to provide a larger range of agricultural occupations and thereby increase production and reduce wastage of time and labour. There are also the village co-operative and the village school, as well as associate bodies like women's and youth organizations and farmers' associations.

In the early days of India's independence the government turned to the important question of how land should be distributed. The system of land holding had been organized in the eighteenth century by the British East India Company. A landed aristocracy had arisen, often absent from the land they owned and taking no interest in its development. This led to the oppression of the peasants and to agrarian troubles. In their first Five-Year Plan, the Indians produced a scheme of land reform. Land, they decided, should properly belong to the person who tills it, and this has remained the ideal ever since. The process of removing the intermediaries who controlled the land but did not work it has been going on ever since. The Bhoodan Movement, begun in 1951, appealed to the landlords voluntarily to give their land away, and as much as 1,800,000 hectares ($4\frac{1}{2}$ million acres) have been collected in this manner.

The clothes worn by people vary according to the part of the country they live in. Generally, though, the men wear a 'dhoti', or loose cotton garment, and

A small village on the banks of the river Cauvery in Madras, southern India

Benares on the River Ganges. Thousands of pilgrims come to pray and to bathe in the waters of this holy city

a loose shirt, while the women usually wear 'saris' and blouses. In some places women wear cotton or silk trousers and a tunic with a small veil round the shoulders or over the head. In the towns, the men sometimes wear semi-Western clothes – jacket, trousers and shirt.

The capital of India is Delhi, which lies on the river Yamuna on the northern part of the plain that separates the Himalayas from the Deccan Plateau. Delhi is really made up of three separate towns – Old Delhi, Cantonment and New Delhi. Much of New Delhi was built by the British, who intended to make the place a splendid capital for the Indian Empire. After the end of the Indian Mutiny in 1858, Delhi was severely punished for her part in the rising; the whole population was forced to leave

165

A village potter making bowls and dishes
An open-air market in southern India

the town and many of the houses were razed to the ground so as to make the defence of the town's fortress easier. Life returned slowly to Delhi after this, and it remained for a long time a provincial town. But in 1877, Queen Victoria had herself proclaimed Empress of India here, and later, in 1911, George V came here to be crowned Emperor.

The continent of India is lucky in being very rich in minerals. Her deposits of iron ore are some of the richest in the world and it is estimated that there are 20,000 million tonnes of coal available for mining. There is also manganese ore and bauxite. The most important mining area includes south Bihar, south-west Bengal and north Orissa. Oil wells have already been sunk in Assam, while prospectors continue to search for further resources in the Punjab, Rajasthan, Gujarat, Uttar Pradesh and West Bengal. There is much light industry – in 1973 India produced $2\frac{1}{2}$ million bicycles, over 2 million electric fans, and $1\frac{1}{2}$ million radio receivers. Her scientists have always been famous, and India's atomic and medical programmes are probably the most advanced in the developing world. But although there are nearly a hundred universities, 25 per cent of the population is illiterate.

India certainly contains much beautiful and varied scenery. Many examples of ancient architecture are still to be found. There are temples, many of which were built out of solid rock or formed by carving the insides of caves, monasteries for Jains or Buddhists, mosques and mausoleums. One of the outstanding monuments is the Lion Capital of Sarnath. It was erected in the third century BC by the Emperor Ashoka to mark the spot where the Buddha first proclaimed his gospel of peace and freedom to the world. On the top of the pillar are the figures of four large lions facing the four corners of the universe and symbolizing power, courage and confidence. Below them, the four directions are guarded by four smaller animals: the lion of the North, the elephant of the East, the horse of the South, and the bull of the West. The last important feature of the pillar is the wheel, or chakra, which is represented in relief. This wheel is also to be found at the centre of the Indian flag, where it is taken to be a symbol of motion or progress.

Ancient buildings are especially noted for the beauty of the stone carving. Sometimes the details of this carving are so delicate that one would think that the craftsman had used ivory instead of stone. Buddhism inspired much of this fine carving, as well as many representations of the Buddha himself. Not all, by any means, of the fine old buildings in India date from this early period. There are many monuments from the Muslim period of Indian history, especially the period of the Moghul Emperors. Perhaps the best known of these outside India is the Taj Mahal, the great tomb built in the seventeenth century, which, it is said, took 20,000 men 22 years to build, not only because of the size of the building but also because of the delicate carving of characters, flowers and abstract patterns that decorate the building.

One would expect such a large country to be full of contrasts, and so it is; contrasts such as that between the pastoral vale of Kashmir in the north and the palm-fringed coasts of the south. In the Himalayas there are hill-stations and holiday

Much new building is going on all over India. This modern development is in Delhi

Terraced gardens in Kashmir, a fertile, mountainous region in the north of India

crocodile appear in the rivers and wild duck and snipe in the marshes. There is also a great variety of birds, some of which, like the Indian bustard, the golden eagle and the red mynah, are becoming very rare and indeed threatened with extinction.

PAKISTAN
Republic
Area: 804,000 sq. km/310,000 sq. miles
Population: 66,800,000   Capital: Islamabad
Flag: Green with white vertical stripes at the mast, the green portion bearing a white crescent in the centre and a 5-pointed heraldic star

Pakistan, once part of Britain's Indian Empire, was constituted as a Dominion in 1947 and became a republic in 1956. There was unrest in the country for some years and in 1971 the area which was then called East Pakistan, and was separated from West Pakistan by over 1,600 km (1,000 miles) of Indian territory, broke away, becoming the independent country of Bangladesh in 1972.

Pakistan, like India, is largely an agricultural country, growing mainly rice, wheat, sugar cane, maize and tobacco, though it is now expanding in the field of drugs, chemicals, iron and steel and manufacturing. Many of the problems of drought, famine and overpopulation are shared by both of these countries.

The principal religion of Pakistan is Islam, over 97 per cent of the population being Muslims. Education is free and compulsory.

BANGLADESH
Republic in Commonwealth
Area: 142,800 sq. km/55,100 sq. miles
Population: 71,600,000   Capital: Dacca
Flag: Green with red disc in centre

Formerly East Pakistan, Bangladesh, under Shaikh Mujibar Rahman, demanded independence in 1970. Civil war broke out between East and West Pakistan and lasted from March to December 1971, when Bangladesh was declared independent. About 80 per cent of the population is employed in agriculture and some 64 per cent of the land is cultivated, most of this being devoted to rice, which is the most important food crop. Sugar cane, wheat and tea are among the other crops grown and Bangladesh supplies 50 per cent of the world's jute.

resorts, where in summer there may be swimming and fishing and in winter skiing and other winter sports. From Darjeeling, on a clear day, there is a magnificent view of the majestic peaks of Mount Everest and Kanchenjunga. There are fine beaches in Madras and Bombay.

Many animals appear in India which are not found in other parts of the world, among them the Indian swamp deer, the brow-antlered deer, the spotted deer, or Chital, the Blue Bull of Nilgai, the Blackbuck and the four-horned antelope. There are also magnificent tigers and, occasionally, the beautiful snow leopard, though this is becoming extremely rare. In the forests there are panthers, bears, wolves and snakes, and monkeys of all kinds; on the plains there are deer and wild boar; trout and

Light industries are expanding and shipping is important, there being two ports, Chittagong and Chalna, and considerable stretches of navigable river. Bangladesh has compulsory primary education and four universities. Disastrous floods followed by famines have resulted in serious loss of life and presented the country with serious problems of rehabilitation and re-housing.

NEPAL
Kingdom
Area: 141,400 sq. km/54,600 sq. miles
Population: 12,000,000   Capital: Katmandu
Flag: Double pennant of crimson edged with blue with symbols of moon and sun in white

To the north of India lies the Kingdom of Nepal, a country which stretches along the southern slopes of the Himalaya Range. The highest mountain in the world, Mount Everest 8,848m (29,028 ft), is situated in Nepal. The capital is Katmandu. The people are mainly either of Mongolian or of Indian origin, and the two main religions are Hinduism and Buddhism. Originally, the people were divided into a number of different hill clans and ruled by princes. One of these clans, the Gurkha, became predominant at the end of the eighteenth century and their ruler founded the present Nepalese dynasty. There are many fertile green valleys sheltered among the high mountains, and crops such as rice, maize and wheat are grown. The lower slopes of the hills are generally covered by jungle. Nepal is able to export, among other things, rice, jute, hides, cattle and timber.

TIBET
Autonomous region of China
Area: 1,222,000 sq. km/472,000 sq. miles
Population: 1,300,000   Capital: Lhasa

Tibet is truly a country on the roof of the world – its average elevation being 4,600m (15,000 ft). Its people are wholly concerned with agriculture, some growing such crops as vegetables, wheat and the like in those areas where cultivation is possible. Others, mainly nomadic, rear such animals as sheep, goats, asses and yaks from which they obtain most of the needs for their meagre existence. Before the Chinese occupied Tibet in 1950 nearly one in five of the adult men were Buddhist monks.

The capital and sacred city of Tibet is Lhasa, the

A Nepalese mountain village in the foothills of the Himalayas. The snow-covered peak on the right is Annapurna

A camel caravan in Afghanistan, a mountainous and arid country. There are fields of barley on either side of the road

home of the Gods, and is some 3,600m (12,000 ft) above sea level. Of the many religious buildings in Lhasa the most spectacular is the Potala Palace, the home of the Dalai Lama until he fled to India in 1959 after revolting against China's influence in Tibet's internal affairs.

BURMA
Republic
Area: 678,000 sq. km/262,000 sq. miles
Population: 29,600,000   Capital: Rangoon
Flag: Red with emblem and stars on blue ground in top corner

Burma is perhaps best described by saying that it

Burmese farmers clear forest areas for growing crops of vegetables, yams and rice. After about seven years the soil is exhausted and another area is burned off

covers the area which is drained by the Irrawaddy river and its tributaries, though part of the course of the Salween, which originates in China, flows through the eastern edge of the country. A trip down the Irrawaddy would reveal the main geographical features of Burma. It begins in the wooded Kachin Heights in the temperate north, not far from the Chinese border. As it flows down into the plain it enters the dry belt of the country, in the region of the old city of Mandalay. In the last part of its course it meanders southwards, splitting eventually into the many separate streams of its delta before it flows into the sea. This vast, flat delta is the granary of Burma, and on its eastern flank stands the capital and chief port of the country, Rangoon.

Burma is primarily an agricultural country, and three-quarters of the population depend on agriculture for their living. Nearly 70 per cent of the cultivable land is used for rice. Most strains of rice only thrive in standing water, so that plenty of rain and efficient irrigation channels are needed if the crop is to be good. Other strains which do not require standing water are used in parts of the Shan Plateau and the other hilly regions. The production of rice on a large scale is a comparatively recent innovation in Burma, for the Burmese rice crop is now ten times what it was in 1866. Enough is pro-

duced to supply the needs of the people as well as to make possible the further export of about a million tonnes.

Large areas in the plains and foothills are covered by deciduous forest, and among these are found the famous hardwoods of Burma, the most important being teak. Teak has been exported from Burma since the sixteenth century, and today it is still the second most important export after rice and other agricultural products. Minerals take third place in the export trade, among them tin and tungsten, silver and lead, and precious stones.

The greater part of Burma lies within the tropics. This means that there is a well-defined monsoon or rainy season, which lasts from the middle of May to the middle of October. In the delta and coastlands this season, with its high temperatures and heavy rain, brings ideal conditions for rice growing, and the climate is humid all the year round. It is very different in the dry zone of central Burma, where the rainfall rarely exceeds 100 cm (40 in) per year, as against 250 cm (100 in) in the Irrawaddy delta. Here the land has to be carefully irrigated if rice is to be grown, but groundnuts, sesame, beans and peas, and cotton and tobacco can also be grown. The farmers in the dry zone generally work small plots which have been in the possession of their families for generations.

Malaya is the richest rubber-growing country in the world. These racks support sheets of rubber for smoking before being exported

MALAYSIA
Nation in Commonwealth
Area: 331,000 sq. km/128,000 sq. miles
Population: 10,400,000
Capital: Kuala Lumpur
Flag: Narrow red and white horizontal stripes with yellow star and crescent on blue ground in top corner

Malaysia is a sovereign State within the Commonwealth and is made up of a Federation of thirteen States. Of these nine have their own Rulers and these elect one of their number to rule as Head of State of the Federation for five years. Most of the States are on the Malay peninsula but in 1963 two others, Sarawak and Sabah (formerly British North Borneo) joined the Federation. For a short period Singapore belonged to the Federation but in 1965 she decided to become independent again. The Federal capital is Kuala Lumpur. Less than half the people of Malaysia are Malays. Most of the remainder are Chinese and there are also many Indians.

A large part of Malaysia is covered with tropical rain forests and those areas which are not are given over to agriculture, especially the growing of rubber trees. Malaysia is the world's largest producer of natural rubber, which is its most important export. Malaysia also supplies one-third of the world's tin.

INDONESIA
Republic
Area: 1,904,000 sq. km/735,000 sq. miles
Population: 124,600,000   Capital: Djakarta
Flag: Equal bands of red over white

The Andaman Sea separates Burma from Sumatra, the nearest of the chain of islands which now forms the Republic of Indonesia. There are over 3,000 of these islands, some large and some small, but the chief ones, apart from Sumatra, are Java, Borneo, the Celebes and Bali. The whole archipelago

A Vietnamese farmer ploughing a rice field

The museum of Pematang in North Sumatra, built in the local style

stretches along the Equator for over 5,000 km (3,000 miles), and forms the connecting link between Asia and Australia.

The most densely populated areas of Indonesia are the islands of Java, Madura and Bali. Here the land is very intensely cultivated, the staple food crop being rice. Nobody can afford to waste land, and so the hillsides are carefully terraced so that even they can bear their crop of rice. In these three areas the rice is generally grown on the 'sawah' principle. The fields are flooded during the growing period and each field is enclosed by a little embankment to prevent the water running off. In areas where there is not enough rainfall to keep the fields flooded, the farmers co-operate in the use of a system of irrigation, but where water is plentiful farmers may produce two crops of rice each year under the 'sawah' system. In some parts of Central Sumatra and other remote areas, the 'landing' system of cultivation is still used, a form of shifting cultivation in which the forest is cleared by burning and planted for two or three years with different

crops before being left fallow again, so that the soil does not become exhausted.

Farming is of two kinds in Indonesia. The peasant farmers run small-scale farms of their own, on which, apart from rice, they produce maize, cassava, sweet potatoes, sago, peanuts and soya-beans, as well as many kinds of fruit. Rubber, sugar, coffee and tobacco are also produced in a small way. In contrast, there are large estates run by the Government which produce a single crop each: rubber, tobacco, sugar, palm-oil, hard fibres, coffee, tea, cocoa or cinchona. Almost all the output of these estates is intended for export.

Seventy per cent of Indonesia's total population live on Java, an elongated island with a central backbone of volcanic mountains, some of which are still active. Between the mountains and the coast there is a fertile alluvial plain, watered by a network of rivers. The high rainfall and rich volcanic soil give rise to luxuriant vegetation. While rice, tea and maize are the most common crops, the gentler climate of the uplands can be used for growing roses, strawberries and other fruits and flowers which are generally associated with temperate climates.

On Java is situated the capital of Indonesia, Djakarta, a city of some 6 million people. From the north to the south of the city is a distance of well over 15 km (10 miles). Like every big, modern city it is crowded with traffic, but here the cars, buses and lorries mix with the characteristic 'betjak', an amalgam of tricycle and cab which is the most popular means of travelling short distances in Djakarta. Scattered throughout the city there are a number of colourful markets, full of a wide variety of goods. Of course, there are department stores and ordinary shops too, but much of the buying and selling takes place in the open-air stalls which the tradesmen set up on the pavements. There are also salesmen who wander from door to door, offering anything and everything for sale: fruit and vege-tables, picture frames, ice-cream and furniture.

It was in this part of the world that one of the most impressive and destructive volcanic explosions of all time took place. In the Sunda Strait, between Java and Sumatra, lies the volcanic island of Krakatoa. In August 1883, the island exploded, leaving only a submarine cavity, and a thick sheet of fragmentary matter across the bed of the sea.

The forests on the surrounding islands were covered by the debris of the explosion and floating larva was carried hundreds of miles on the surface of the ocean. Perhaps the most remarkable feature was the effect of the dust which the explosion released into the air. Djakarta is 150 km (100 miles) from Krakatoa, yet at midday on the day of the explosion the dust was so thick over the city that the lamps had to be lighted. At Bandung, which is 100 km (70 miles) further away and 100m (2,300 ft) above sea level, the sun was obscured for a time. Some of the dust was even blown high into the upper atmosphere, and the tiny particles were the cause of the beautiful sunrises and sunsets which were seen all over Europe at the time. The sound of the explosion was heard almost 5000 km (3,000 miles) away, and many people heard it in Bangkok in Thailand, in the Philippines, in Ceylon, and in West and South Australia. The explosion produced a succession of mammoth waves, some of which even affected seas as distant as the English Channel.

CHINA
Republic
Area: 9,561,000 sq. km/3,692,000 sq. miles
Population: 814,300,000   Capital: Peking
Flag: Red with gold star and 4 smaller stars in top left-hand corner

China has the largest population in the world. The Chinese have a recorded history dating back to 2200 BC. The nation developed largely in isolation from the rest of the world, and it is for this reason that so much in Chinese life and Chinese thinking is difficult to understand. The Chinese have for centuries regarded other nations with suspicion and held that the quality of life outside China could by no means match up to their own. It was quite reasonable for them to hold these opinions, for the western countries that had wielded power and influence when China was a young nation had long since passed away. Classical Chinese literature, for example, flourished in the third and fourth centuries BC, nearly 2,000 years before the great period in European literature began. In the nineteenth century, trade brought the Chinese more and more into contact with other nations, but this did not in the long run make for more harmonious relations; like others in Asia and Africa, they resented the foreigners who lived on their soil, made profits

from their trade, and all to frequently imposed unfair treaties upon them.

As China moved into the twentieth century, she slowly began to realize how important the industrial arts that the West had mastered were to become and since 1949, when the communists took over power, more and more attention was paid to developing the country industrially. Yet the aloofness from the Western countries continued, perhaps because the Chinese political system is in such complete contrast to the systems favoured in Western Europe and North America. Even the Russians, whose revolution in 1917 provided the inspiration for the Chinese communist forces during their fight with the old National government in the late 1940's, and

A new railway bridge over the Yellow River

A farming commune near Canton in southern China. The crop in the foreground is rice; sugar cane is growing behind, on the left

173

The Far East

U. S. S. R.

L.Baikal

• Khabarovsk

SAKHALIN

MONGOLIA

• Ulan Bator

MANCHURIA

GOBI DESERT

HOKK

JAPAN

SINKIANG

INNER MONGOLIA

• Harbin

Vladivostok

Sapporo

Shenyang

N. KOREA

Sea of Japan

Great Wall of China

• Peking

Tientsin

Pyongyang

HONSHU

Kunlun Mts.

Taiyuan

Seoul

S. KOREA

Fuji 12390 ▲ • Tokyo • Yokohama

Hwang Ho (Yellow River)

Tsingtao

Hiroshima

Osaka

TIBET

• Sian

Great Plain of China

Yellow Sea

Nagasaki

SHIKOKU

KYUSHU

PEOPLE'S REPUBLIC OF CHINA

Nanking

Lhasa • Namcha Barwa ▲ 25445

• Chengtu

• Wuhan

Shanghai

East China Sea

Chungking

Yangtze Kiang

INDIA

Yunnan Plateau

BANGLADESH

Taipeh

Dacca

Si Kiang

Canton

Tropic of Cancer

1

BURMA

Irrawaddy

Salween

Mandalay

Hanoi

Hong Kong

PACIFIC OCEAN

Rangoon

Vientiane

LAOS

Mekong

HAI NAN

Gulf of Tonkin

LUZON

THAILAND

Bangkok

Angkor

KHMER REP.

VIETNAM

Manila

PHILIPPINE ISLANDS

Andaman Is.

Andaman Sea

Phnom Penh

Saigon

South China Sea

Gulf of Thailand

Sulu Sea

MINDANAO

Kota Kinabalu

MALAYA

SABAH

Celebes Sea

Strait of Malacca

Kuala Lumpur

MALAYSIA

2

3

SARAWAK

Kuching

SUMATRA

Equator

BORNEO (KALIMANTAN)

SULAWESI

IRI JA

JAVA

INDONESIA

| 0 | 500 | 1000 miles |
| 0 | 500 | 1000 | 1500 kilometres |

1 TAIWAN
2 BRUNEI
3 SINGAPORE

Attending a flock of geese on a Chinese commune

who gave so much encouragement to the Chinese communists in the early days, did not maintain these close relations. However, much more communication is now taking place between China and the Western powers.

One of the factors that has discouraged contacts between China and the West has been her language. There are a vast number of dialects, which more or less amount to separate languages, the most important of which is Mandarin. The communists have used Mandarin as the basis for what they call the Common Speech, which is intended to become the national language of China, though people will probably continue to use their local dialect as well. Nevertheless, there are obvious advantages in having a language which foreigners can be sure will be understood in every part of the country and which make communication easy even in the most distant parts of this vast country.

The Chinese written language is also in process of simplification. Chinese has no alphabet: there is no use of combinations of letters to describe a sound, as in the majority of languages in the world. Chinese characters are used to convey meaning, not sound. The system of Arabic numerals which we use is rather similar. The figure '8' means the same both to a Frenchman and to an Englishman (or anyone else), though in French it is pronounced 'huit' and in English 'eight'. In Chinese, 'salt' is represented by a character, a tiny drawing made up of a number of strokes. A Chinese will understand that this character means 'salt' whatever dialect he speaks, though if he were to pronounce the word it would sound quite different in different dialects. In the early days of Chinese writing, each character was, in fact, a miniature drawing of the object to be described; as the years passed, these drawings became more complex as more and more objects had characters assigned to them. Abstract ideas had to be represented too. The drawings gradually became formalized, and were no longer recognizable as representations of the objects they described, but they remained complex: the character for 'salt', for example, needs twenty-four pen strokes.

Harvesting tea on an upland plantation in China

Teams of labourers working on the Hwang Ho dam in China

A busy river scene; in parts of China boats are often used as homes

The advantages of characters over an alphabet are obvious. When one man met another who spoke a quite different dialect that he could not understand, he could communicate by drawing characters in the air, or scratching them in the dust on the ground. But the disadvantages are even greater. Every object and idea had to have a distinctive character, with the result that the number of characters ran into thousands; so many thousands, in fact, that scholars have never been able to agree on exactly how many Chinese characters there are, though the figure is something between forty and fifty thousand. Not only did it require great powers of memory to learn enough characters to read classical Chinese, but writing was very slow and the typesetting of books extremely complicated. Reading and writing became the privilege of a tiny minority of the people.

This problem, too, has been tackled. Many of the most important characters have been simplified, so that they continue to convey the same idea, but can be written with half the number of strokes. Even so, it was seen that this would not be sufficient if everyone was to learn to read and write without spending too much time over it. An alphabet, based on our own Latin alphabet, has been drawn up, and is being used to help children to learn how to pronounce the characters in the Common Speech.

China is still essentially an agricultural country, and the cultivation of the soil is now done on a

communal basis. The whole rural population is divided into some 74,000 communes – which roughly correspond in size to large townships – which are in turn divided into production teams and brigades, composed of about forty-five families. Before the Revolution in 1949, land was owned by a comparatively small number of landowners, while the vast majority of people owned nothing and were constantly in debt to their landlords who took percentages of their crops. This would have been a miserable enough situation for the peasants; but it was aggravated by shortage of land – only one-ninth of China's land area was, until recently, arable – and unpredictable weather conditions. A man who might struggle to live and keep his family when there was plenty of rain for the rice would be ruined when the drought caused his crops to fail, for he had nothing to fall back on; being constantly in debt to his landlord he could never save up enough to pull him through a lean year.

The strongest appeal of the Revolution to the people was that it was determined to remedy this situation; only those who tilled the land should own it, it maintained. As the communists took over each area, the land was confiscated and shared out between the peasants. Each landlord was left with a small piece of his former land which he could cultivate if he wished, like the other peasants. When the communists had taken control of the whole country, they began the 'land reform', in which the

Ploughing the rice fields ready for planting on a commune in Yunnan in south China

A winter view of the administrative centre of Peking

land was distributed as fairly as possible among the entire peasant population.

This was only the first stage in the reform of Chinese rural life, for it was seen that real progress in agriculture could only be made if new equipment were introduced and the land improved. Though the peasants now owned their own land, and could take what profits from it they could earn, without the interference of a landlord, yet there were still many people to feed off too little soil, and money could never be laid aside for investment in machinery. Irrigation programmes and the reclaiming of hillside land by terracing were urgently needed, but they required large numbers of people working together. The farmers were accordingly encouraged to join mutual aid teams, and to pool their resources to buy equipment and to improve the land, and this gradually developed into co-operative farming.

Even these measures, however, turned out to be insufficient to deal with China's enormous need for food. Men were also being wasted, lying idle because there was nothing for them to do. The situation was better than it had been before the Second World War, when, on average, men only worked for about 130 days per year, but there was still a lot of untapped labour. The turning point came during the government's drive in 1957–8 to increase cultivable land and improve irrigation. Millions of people, both from the country and the towns, came to lend a hand in building dams, digging new irrigation canals and sinking new wells. The work added another $5\frac{1}{4}$ million hectares (13 million acres) to the country's cultivable area, but it also showed the people of the co-operatives how much they would benefit by belonging to an even larger unit than they did already. Just as they had joined up to build dams, so they could also pool their spare labour and plant trees, or open mines, and pool their spare capital to buy machinery that required a very large outlay.

In the late 1950's, co-operatives began to join together and call themselves 'communes', following the example set by some co-operatives in Honan Province. The peasants there divided themselves up into groups to deal with the various tasks that had to be done; while the woman also joined in the work, when they had arranged for their children to be looked after in nurseries. From this the idea of the commune developed, organized by elected leaders and run according to its own set of by-laws. The commune today does not just mean the convenient arrangement of the labour force within each area so as to make the best out of the land; it is a whole community, with schools (both for children and adults), factories, hospitals and canteens. All the duties that in Western Europe rest on the Local Authorities and leaders of industry are in China part of the offices of the commune or, as the organizing body is known, local Revolutionary Committee.

Rice remains the staple food of the Chinese. In the north, cereal crops such as maize, wheat, barley and millet are grown, together with peas and beans. Cotton is an important crop, though China does not produce enough for her own needs, and is grown mainly in the Yangtze and Yellow River valleys. Tea is grown in the west and south of the country. China is fortunate in being very rich in minerals – not only is coal of very high quality produced, but also tin and iron ore. Oil is being produced in a number of provinces.

The ancient city of Peking has once again been restored to its position as capital of China. There was already a settlement where Peking stands today more than 4,000 years ago. It has been burnt, sacked, damaged by earthquakes, and many times overrun by foreign powers. Kublai Khan completely rebuilt the city.

The old part of the city, which still remains, was built in a very formal pattern – rectangular, and enclosed in a series of walls. Having passed through the wall of the Chinese city, the wall of the Tartar city, and the wall of the Imperial City one comes eventually to the wall of the Imperial Palace and the Forbidden City. From here, the Emperors ruled the vast land of China. Though there are no longer any Emperors, the gardens, courtyards and perfectly proportioned palaces with their golden roofs have been preserved. The Forbidden City is now open to anyone who pays the small admission fee.

But Peking is more than just the old city. In 1949, it was mainly enclosed within the old walls, but since then it has expanded in every direction. The population of Peking is now almost four times as large as it was when the communists first entered the city. Large buildings have been erected with almost incredible rapidity. The buildings bordering Tien An Men Square, which covers nearly 40

Working in an engineering factory in China

Junks on the Yangtze River in China

hectares (100 acres), are some of the most impressive. To the east of the Square is the new Museum of Chinese History, containing beautifully displayed objects from every period. Opposite the Museum is the Great Hall of the People, a simple elegant building of massive proportions. Its frontage is 330m (1,100 ft) long, and the banqueting hall within can seat up to 5,000 people. It contains also an auditorium, known as the Great Hall, which holds 10,000; here the political rallies are held.

In 1949, after many years of civil war, communications in China had practically broken down, but since then a considerable effort has been made to extend an efficient communications system to every part of the country. The rivers remain an important part of the transport system between east and west – the Yangtze, for example, is 5,520 km (3,430 miles) long, and the Yellow River 4,672 km (2,903 miles) – but have now been overshadowed by more rapid and modern lines of communication. What is more, the mountainous areas of western China – about half the country – have now received their fair share of roads, railways and airports, in spite of the difficulty of the terrain; formerly the lowland east was the only area that was at all well provided for. Compared with 1949, the length of railway track has been increased by about 50 per cent, the length of road is five times as great, and there are over 150,000 km (100,000 miles) of inland waterways, or twice as much as in 1949. Internal air routes, providing a rapid and cheap means of travel over mountainous terrain, have been extended to many parts of the country.

HONG KONG
UK Dependent Territory
Area: 1,030 sq. km/398 sq. miles
Population: 4,100,000   Capital: Hong Kong
Flag: Blue ground with Union Jack against mast and coat-of-arms on white disc
Only two foreign enclaves remain on the Chinese mainland: Macao, which belongs to Portugal, and Hong Kong, a British Crown Colony.

Hong Kong consists of some islands and a small part of the mainland on the eastern side of the estuary of the Pearl River. The total area is 1,030 sq. km (398 sq. miles), and the population fluctuates considerably owing to the number of Chinese who move back and forth across the Chinese border. The island of Hong Kong, first occupied by Britain in 1841, covers an area of 78 sq. km (30 sq. miles), and the capital city, Victoria, is situated on its northern side. At one point, the island is only 450m (500 yd) away from the mainland, and between Victoria and the mainland lies the famous harbour, which was the main reason for the rapid development of this outlying colony. Here vessels of up to 250m (800 ft) can draw up to the wharves and a terminal for ocean-going ships has also been constructed. There are modern dockyards and dry docks that can take both bulk oil tankers and ocean-going liners. Opposite Victoria on the mainland is the city of Kowloon, which has a population as large as that of the capital. Kowloon was acquired under the Peking Convention in 1860. The New Territories occupy a peninsula in the southern part of the Kwangtung Province of China and some off-shore islands. China leased them to Britain at the end of the nineteenth century, and the lease is due to run out in 1997.

Mountains in the New Territories reach up over 910m (3,000 ft), and the island of Hong Kong is dominated by the 550m (1,800 ft) high Victoria Peak. Average temperatures are 15 deg. C. in February and 28 deg. C. in July, and the winters are much drier than the summers, three-quarters of the rain falling between May and September, the period of the monsoon.

Hong Kong is an important stopping-off point not only for the large passenger ships and the commercial vessels, but also for aircraft. Planes bound for Korea, Tokyo, the Philippines, Australia, Singapore, and Thailand call here, and the twin cities of Kowloon and Victoria provide plenty of entertainment, bustling markets and shops for any-one who takes some time off here.

Because of her excellent position on the trade routes, Hong Kong originally gained much of her wealth merely as a trading centre, importing goods from one country and re-exporting them to another; but today, though this kind of trade is still import-ant, Hong Kong has also become an important manufacturer, and many of the cheap goods made here find their way to many parts of the western world. Transistor radios and other electrical goods made in Hong Kong are familiar, as is jewellery, a

Junks are still built by the traditional methods; here is one under construction in Hong Kong

The waterfront of Hong Kong seen from Kowloon

A busy market street in Hong Kong

the whole landscape is dominated by the mountains, especially Mt. Fuji at 3,776m (12,388 ft). Mt. Fuji has not erupted since 1707, but there are still 58 active volcanoes. The hot springs that are a feature of these volcanic areas were once used in the treatment of the sick, but today they feed the hot-spring resorts where Japanese holiday makers go in search of rest.

The population density of Japan is almost 300 persons per sq. km. The capital city of Tokyo now has a population of more than eleven million. More and more Japanese are leaving the countryside and going to live in the towns and cities where there are more jobs available and the pay is better. The pace of life is much more rapid in the towns, where new blocks for European-style offices, stores or flats are going up all the time.

There are still about 6½ million Japanese who work full-time on the land, though others do not spend all their time on their farms but have part-time jobs in the factories. Japanese farms are still very small, just as they were in the past, when everybody was dependent on agriculture for their living and there was only a little arable land to go round. Two-and-a-half acres is an average size for a Japanese farm. But, because there is so little land, every square inch that there is is put to good use. Even the hills and the smaller mountains are put under cultivation by carving row upon row of terraces out of the mountainside. Terracing and the small size of the farms used to make it difficult to use tractors and other kinds of farm machinery, but new mechanical aids have recently been developed – mechanical tillers, for example – which are a great help to the small farmer and are now extensively used. Farming is much easier in Hokkaido, where good arable land is quite plentiful.

The main crop in Japan is rice, and, thanks to the use of machinery and fertilizers and the development of new strains of rice, Japanese farms are among the most productive rice-producing units in the world. The rice-crop from an acre of Japanese land is about three times as great as that in most other Asian countries. Other crops are wheat and barley. Farmers keep comparatively few animals in Japan because there is so little good pasture land, but some dairy and beef cattle are kept, as well as pigs and chickens. Silkworms are still kept in Japan, though fewer than before, but fruit growing

wide range of plastic goods, and cotton, silk and rayon. Printing is also an important industry.

JAPAN
Democratic State with Emperor
Area: 370,000 sq. km/143,000 sq. miles
Population: 108,700,000   Capital: Tokyo
Flag: White with red sun in centre
Japan consists of four main islands – Honshu (Mainland), Shikoku, Kyushu and Hokkaida – and thousands of smaller islands that stretch along the Pacific Coast of the Asian mainland for some 2,500 km (1,500 miles). Japan lies in the temperate zone, so there is plenty of rainfall and the climate is generally mild. There is a rainy season towards the beginning of June that usually lasts for about four weeks, and is then followed by a warm humid summer. The winter is usually mild with plenty of sunny days, though there is heavy snow in the northern part of the country. Though, thanks to the climate, there is plenty of lush, green countryside,

A beautiful example of traditional Japanese architecture

A typical Japanese coastal fishing village. Fish is an essential part of Japan's food supply

is on the increase. Many Japanese mandarin oranges and peaches are exported to countries in Europe.

In Japan, wood is still the main building material in the countryside (though no longer in the towns) and, in the form of charcoal, is widely used for cooking and heating in rural districts. These needs are supplied partly by the natural forests found on the islands and partly by specially planted forests which account for about one-third of the total forest area. Japan has also become a big importer of timber, for she needs a great deal of wood-pulp for her paper mills.

The Japanese have been a fishing people through-out their history, and today fishing still provides an important part of their food-supply. Indeed, they catch about 16 per cent of the world's total, more than any other single country. There are three kinds of fishing in Japan – coastal fishing, offshore fishing, and deep-sea fishing. Coastal fishing can be carried on by boats of up to ten tons, or by fixed nets in coastal waters, or by breeding fish artificially in shallow waters, which is called fish-farming. Prawns, sea-bream and yellowtails are all bred by

this last method, which has brought a tremendous increase in the number of fish available in Japanese shops. The offshore fishing boats are generally of about 10 to 100 tonnes, while deep-sea fishing is carried on in much larger vessels. The trawlers that fish off the African coast, for example, are generally of about 2,000 to 3,000 tonnes, and the tuna fishing ships of about 200 to 500 tonnes. Japanese ships go to the north Pacific to catch salmon and crab and to the Antarctic Ocean to catch whales. In both cases, large fleets are used, centred on a mother ship which can process and tin the catch while still at sea, so that the ships which do the catching do not waste time returning to their home port.

Less than one per cent of the houses in Japan are without electricity, thanks to the fact that the natural resources of the country are well situated for the production of electricity. Deep valleys and heavy rainfall have made it comparatively easy to produce a highly efficient hydro-electric network. But this is not the only way that power is produced in Japan. Thirteen nuclear power stations are now in operation.

The resurgence of Japanese industry since the

end of the Second World War probably could not have taken place had it not been for the rapid expansion of the basic industries, notably the iron and steel industry. Though the industry depends heavily on imports of foreign iron ore, scrap iron and coking coal, production of steel, for example, has increased ten times over the last sixteen years, making Japan the third largest producer in the world after the United States and the Soviet Union.

There are now few parts of the world that are not familiar with at least one kind of Japanese mass-produced machinery, and even countries in Europe, which make their own cars, sewing-machines and transistor-radios, are finding that Japanese products are competing with their own produce in their home markets. The efficiency of Japanese manufacturing techniques and the availability of manpower enable the Japanese to produce these items more cheaply than similar items can be produced in other countries. This seems to be particularly true in the motor industry. Serious production of motor-cars began in Japan in the early 1950's, and the industry has developed fast, making well-designed models that compare favourably in speed, comfort and

efficiency with the cars produced in France, West Germany and Britain. Japan is now the second largest passenger-car producer in the world, and Japanese cars and motor-cycles are a familiar sight.

Japan is now the leading shipbuilding nation in the world, and also produces the world's largest ships, especially oil-tankers. Their success has been largely due to their technical know-how and application. They have building docks which can hold 200,000-tonne vessels, and their docks are put to their maximum use by beginning on the building of the next ship in the same dock before the previous one is finished. Automated and remote-controlled machinery is also used.

One of the most impressive Japanese achievements is the streamlining of her railway system, which is still a very important form of transport in the country, especially for goods. Japan National Railways runs the fastest train service in the world from Tokyo to the important industrial centre of Osaka and beyond to Okayama, 161 km (101 miles) in 58 minutes over the latter part of the journey.

Almost every western sport is played in Japan, but there are also the traditional Japanese sports

Mount Fuji, Japan's sacred mountain. It is a volcano, but is thought now to be extinct as it has not erupted for many years

like sumo wrestling, judo, karate and kendo, or Japanese fencing. Sumo wrestling is claimed to be more than 2,000 years old, and the object of each wrestler is to force his opponent to the ground or out of the ring. Judo was developed from the old art known as jujitsu, and is now a popular sport not only in Japan but also in many western countries. Judo is a form of self-defence which requires quick thinking and rapid action rather than great strength or size. It was included in the Olympic Games for the first time in 1964. Karate originated in China and is a style of fighting which uses all the limbs of the body for defence and attack. Kendo is Japan's traditional form of fencing in which split bamboo poles are used rather than the fencing swords or foils which we use. The sport is now becoming popular again.

Though the pace of life in Japan is now as rapid as that in any of the western countries, some of the ceremonial of the old Japanese way of life remains. There is, for example, the traditional art of flower arrangement, which the Japanese, both men and women, regard as a serious and artistic pursuit. But probably the most formal feature of Japanese life, and the one that is least easily understood, is the Tea Ceremony (chanoyu). The history of the Tea Ceremony goes back a long way. Tea was introduced into Japan in about AD 700 from China, but in the twelfth century it was still very rare and precious and was used mostly as a medicine rather than as a beverage. The Zen Buddhist priests found that it helped them to keep awake during their long hours of meditation. During the fourteenth century tea became popular at last and tea plantations began to flourish in Japan. A game was introduced from China called *tocha*, in which the guests were served with several cups of tea produced in different regions, and were asked to choose which contained the tea grown in the best tea-growing area. Those who guessed correctly were given prizes. Gradually this occasion became more formal. This was at a time when the *samurai*, or warrior-class, were the most influential people in the land, and their formal way of life affected everything. Prizes were no longer awarded, but certain formal rules and procedures were introduced which had to be followed, and the influence of Zen Buddhism also came into play, for the object of the ceremony was now to create a peaceful and contemplative atmosphere. By the time the ceremony was perfected in the sixteenth-century it had come to include more than just tea-drinking. Apart from the pleasure involved in the discipline required in taking part in such a rigidly formal ceremony, it was also necessary that the ceremony should take place in a suitable setting – in a room that was plain but beautiful, outside which was a garden where the guests could sit during the pause in the ceremony. On the walls there would be well-chosen hanging-scrolls or a flower arrangement, and the utensils for tea would be of the best. All this was an encouragement towards perfection for Japanese architecture, landscape gardening, pottery and flower arrangement.

Buddhism is the major religion in Japan. It came to Japan around the middle of the sixth century from India through China and Korea. It has been important both as a religion and as a source of developing art and learning throughout Japanese history. Shintoism, which is not strictly a religion, exists side by side with Buddhism in Japanese life. The cult is concerned with the worship of the ancestors of the Emperor and of the ancestors of the individual families. Many Japanese go through Shinto rites when they marry, but when they die, Buddhist funeral rites are performed over them. Christianity was brought to Japan in 1549 by St. Francis Xavier, a Jesuit missionary. Though it spread rapidly at first it was later proscribed, and Christian ceremonies were not allowed again until the middle of the nineteenth century. There are now both Protestants and Catholics. Confucianism is a code of behaviour, not a religion, and has been very influential throughout the greater part of Japanese history. Introduced into Japan at the beginning of the sixth century, it was a guiding influence over Japanese thought and behaviour until the Second World War.

Japan is well known for her theatre, especially the three Japanese forms of classical drama – the Noh plays, the Banraku puppet drama and Kabuki theatre. Noh is a highly stylized dramatic form dating back to the thirteenth century. It was originally performed only for the upper classes, and was derived from rituals and religious dances.

A farming area in a fertile valley in a mountainous region of Japan

Kanmon Grand Bridge, one of the many new engineering projects in Japan

The Bunraku puppet drama dates back to the sixteenth century, and is performed regularly in Osaka. The puppets are half life-size and are elaborately decorated. They may be controlled by one, two or three puppeteers. Accompanied by music and a spoken narrative, human emotion can be very convincingly created by the clever use of these puppets. Kabuki is probably Japan's most famous dramatic form. This developed in the seventeenth century, borrowing both from Noh and Banraku, and from the theatrical arts of an earlier age. In the earliest days it was performed by a troupe of women and later by young men. Today, only men perform in Kabuki plays.

PHILIPPINES
Republic
Area: 300,000 sq. km/116,000 sq. miles
Population: 40,200,000   Capital: Quezon City
Flag: Blue and red horizontal bands with sun and three stars on white triangle

The Philippines are a collection of small islands on the edge of the Pacific Ocean. To the west and north of the islands is the China Sea separating them from the mainland of China, to the south is the Sulu Sea and the Celebes Sea beyond which lie the islands of Celebes and Borneo. In the Republic of the Philippines there are roughly 7,107 islands. Most of these are far too small to show on the map,

Drying fishing nets on one of the Fijian islands

A village of thatched huts, typical of buildings throughout the Pacific islands

Coconuts are harvested for their kernels which, when dried, are known as 'copra' and used in the making of such things as soap and margarine

but if you look carefully at a large-scale map you will be able to see the large number of small black dots around the main islands which are called Luzon and Mindanao. Luzon has a land area of 108,400 sq. km (41,800 sq. miles) and the area of Mindanao is 94,200 sq. km (36,400 sq. miles); the other islands of any size are Samar Negros, Palawan, Panay, Mindoro, Leyte, Cebu, Bohol, and Masbate. No one is ever certain of the exact number of islands within the Philippines because many of them are still active volcanoes. From time to time an island sinks in a volcanic eruption below the sea or a new island is thrown up. In many cases the new island is just a bare rock, too small for any kind of human or animal life and it may vanish as quickly and unexpectedly as it came.

The country is made up of high mountains with rich valleys and wide plains in which farming employs some eight million people out of the total labour force of twelve million. Although the output of agriculture, notably sugar, has increased rapidly, by nearly 50 per cent in the last ten years, the country does not produce enough cereal food for its needs and has to import large quantities. In 1973 food imports included over 100 million US dollars' worth of rice and corn. The reason for this food shortage is not the usual one in a small island; there is plenty of land and farming methods are fairly modern. The main problem is that a very high proportion of the population are too young to work in the production of food. The main agricultural exports are the products of the coconut tree, oil, meal, desiccated coconut and fibres. The largest product is sugar, which is exported only to the United States where demand is enough to use the entire crop. Molasses are exported mainly to Japan, which lies north of the Philippines. Manila hemp which was once a very important export crop is not as thriving as it used to be because of the competition from man-made synthetic fibres and cheaper African sisal. Fruit, tobacco and rubber are the other main exports; rubber, in particular, is increasing in quantity and soon the crop is expected to meet both home and export demands.

However, the main export from the Philippines is timber and timber products. A large part of the area of the islands is covered with dense forests. Most wood goes to Japan and the United States, especially veneers and plywood; one of the most important trees is a hardwood known as Philippine mahogany, but altogether there are over 3,000 varieties of trees in the islands of which about 1,000 are grown commercially. A great deal of fishing is done from the coasts of the islands and fish forms a very important part of the diet of most Filipinos. As well as sea fishing a great deal of inland fishing is done from specially stocked fishponds to provide fresh fish for people living far from the sea.

The publisher wishes to thank the following sources for permission
to reproduce the colour photographs which illustrate this work.
Almasy; Andreb; Atlas; Australian News and Information
Bureau; Beauchene; Bellair; British Petroleum Company; British
Travel Authority; CCD; Chardin; Peter Cobb; Cochet; Demesse;
Dempster; Dupaquier; Eisenkopf; Doc Frse; Goldner; Grelier;
Grevin; Hetier; High Commissioner for New Zealand; Holmes-
Lebel; Hong Kong Government Tourist Office; Idoux; Indian
Tourist Authority; Japanese Tourist Authority; Journot;
Lagraulet; Landry; Langlais; Le Brec; Le Lannou; Lockwood
Survey Corporation; Marty; Merckx; Micaud; Morance; Naud;
Nicolas; Oxo; Ozzello; Perceval; Phototheque-Lapie; Pictor;
Pierre; Pitie; Riboud-Magnum; Robillard; Rougeron; Rouquet;
Service de Presse Sovietique; Spirale; Stevens; Tony Stone
Associates; Suinot; Tazieff; U.S.I.S.; Vasselet; Villaret;
Villemino; Vincent; Wagner.

Index